FROM ZERO TO FOUR FIGURES
MAKING $1,000 A MONTH SELF-PUBLISHING FICTION

PAUL AUSTIN ARDOIN

CONTENTS

Introduction: Who Should Read This Book? ix

PART ONE
SATISFYING BOOKS

1. THE PESKY SIX-YEAR-OLD 3
2. WHY I CHOSE TO SELF-PUBLISH 13
3. SETTING YOUR EXPECTATIONS 18
   Your expectations to get to $1,000 a month 19
   Don't expect overnight success 20
   Know your goals 21
   Your author business is a business 22
4. MEETING READER EXPECTATIONS 25
   The importance of readers' expectations 25
   Think like your reader 27
   How readers find books 28
   Making decisions about the books you write 29
   Genre: categorizing your books 30
   Targeting the right audience: choosing a primary genre 31
   Genre mash-ups 33
   Genre: deciding whether to write to market 35
   Genre: make sure readers know what to expect 37
   Titles, covers, and descriptions 37
   Series or standalone? 38

The power of a series	40
Book or story length	41

5. MY EXPERIENCE WITH READER EXPECTATIONS IN MY BOOKS — 43
- Success: The Fenway Stevenson Mysteries — 43
- Failure: Bad Weather — 44
- Fiasco: The romance books — 46
- Saving a failure: Murders of Substance — 52
- My failures in perspective — 58

6. GETTING YOUR MANUSCRIPT READY TO PUBLISH — 59
- What does editing entail? — 59
- One: The self-edit — 60
- Two: Alpha reader — 61
- Three: Developmental edit — 62
- Four: Beta readers and sensitivity reader — 63
- Five: Line/copy edit — 64
- Six: Proofread — 64
- Seven: Read it out loud — 64

7. THE COST OF RUNNING YOUR AUTHOR BUSINESS — 66
- The cost of creating your draft — 67
- The cost of your final manuscript — 67
- The cost of converting your final manuscript to a sellable book — 68
- Creating an ebook — 69
- Creating other formats — 70
- My experience: the cost of creating my first novel — 76

PART TWO
EFFECTIVE MARKETING

8. YOUR BOOK IS AN ADVERTISEMENT,
   NOT A PRODUCT 81
   Product sampling as advertising 86
   Product sampling for authors: fewer
   downsides 89
   The ad is important, but the quality of
   the book is crucial 91

9. TURNING YOUR BOOK INTO AN
   ADVERTISEMENT 94
   Step One: The Hook 94
   Step Two: The Look 97

10. SPENDING MONEY TO MAKE MONEY 99

11. WHERE WILL YOU SELL YOUR BOOKS? 101
    KU or wide? 102
    How does KU work? 102
    How does an author go wide? 104
    Recommendations: KU vs. Wide 106

12. PROMOTING YOUR BOOK 109
    The importance of covers 110
    Getting your book in front of readers 112
    Make it easy for readers to get your
    next book 112
    Newsletter lists 112
    Creating an effective newsletter 113
    Building a newsletter list: BookFunnel
    and StoryOrigin 115
    Other ways to attract newsletter
    subscribers 117
    What if you hate making newsletters? 117
    The cost of email newsletters 118

Advertising in paid promo newsletters — 119
Advertising on Facebook, Amazon, and BookBub — 122

13. FIGURING OUT WHICH PROMOTIONS WORK — 124
    Separate your promotions — 124
    Noise in the data — 129
    Making decisions with incomplete information — 131

14. PRICING: STRATEGY AND BALANCE — 133
    My pricing strategy — 133
    Pricing high or low — 134
    Selling at 99¢ — 135
    Selling for free — 136
    When to go free — 138
    Selling for different prices across different stores — 139
    Figuring out your price — 141

15. STARTING WITH NO MONEY — 143

PART THREE
PUTTING IT ALL TOGETHER

16. PRIORITIZE — 153
    Focus on the product first — 153

17. PLAN AND EXECUTE — 157
    Balancing marketing and writing — 157
    Getting started with marketing: BookFunnel or StoryOrigin — 158

18. A SAMPLE TIMELINE TO GET TO $1,000 A MONTH — 161
    Month 1 — 162
    Month 2 — 163

Month 3	163
Troubleshooting: What happens if this isn't working?	164
Are you not getting downloads on your Entry Point Novel?	165
Are you getting downloads, but not getting readthrough to Book 2?	166
Months 4-8	168
Month 9	168
Month 10: Seems like a setback	169
Month 11	170
Troubleshooting: What happens if your paid newsletter promos don't work?	170
Months 12-15	171
Month 16	172
Month 17	172
Month 18+	173
Can It Really Work Like This?	173
19. KEEP GOING!	175
Glossary	179
Acknowledgments	183
Mystery Fiction by Paul Austin Ardoin	185

FROM ZERO TO FOUR FIGURES: MAKING $1,000 A MONTH SELF-PUBLISHING FICTION

Copyright © 2023 Paul Austin Ardoin

All rights reserved.

ISBN 978-1-949082-47-0

No parts of this publication may be reproduced, stored in a retrieval system, or transmitted in any form or by any means, electronic, mechanical, photocopying, recording, or otherwise, without the prior written permission of the copyright owner.

This book is sold subject to the condition that it shall not, by way of trade or otherwise, be lent, resold, hired out, or otherwise circulated without the publisher's prior consent in any form of binding or cover other than that in which it is published and without a similar condition including this condition being imposed on the subsequent purchaser. Under no circumstances may any part of this book be photocopied for resale.

This is a work of fiction. Any similarity between the characters and situations within its pages and places or persons, living or dead, is unintentional and coincidental.

Cover design by Ziad Ezzat of Feral Creative Colony

Edited by Max Christian Hansen

Information about the author can be found at http://www.paulaustinardoin.com

INTRODUCTION: WHO SHOULD READ THIS BOOK?

Many experts have written books about being successful in self-publishing. This book is different in that it focuses on two attainable goals for authors at the beginning of the bookselling journey: How to make $1,000 a month in profit, and how to set up your approach to book writing for success throughout your career.

So many books that promise ways to make $100,000 per year or more can seem daunting—and many of them focus solely on marketing. As mystery author G.B. Ralph says, "Those books feel like a ridiculous, unattainable leap when you're currently only selling a handful of copies to supportive friends and family."

But anyone with a marketing degree knows that the product—in this case, your novels—must not only be high-quality, but must fill a need. That's why this book also discusses how to create books that sell. You can't be successful selling a great book without good marketing, and you can't successfully market a book that doesn't give your audience what it wants.

If your aim is $1,000 a month, you must achieve two goals. Goal 1: Create books that will satisfy readers. Goal 2: Get those books into their hands through effective marketing.

WHY $1,000 A MONTH?

Many book marketing experts talk about much loftier goals than $1,000 a month. After all, $1,000 a month isn't enough to quit your day job. So why start there?

In my experience, I've found that most authors who aren't yet making much money are wary of investing in some of the bigger, more expensive marketing tools and strategies. Many authors don't have (or are unwilling to spend) thousands of dollars every month to promote their books—especially when they don't know what works yet.

$1,000 a month is a more realistic goal, and there are less expensive tools and less time-consuming strategies that will allow you to figure out what about your writing is working, what isn't working, and where to refocus your writing energies.

Another reason to choose the goal of $1,000 a month is that once you reach that goal, you'll have both the knowledge and the money to invest in some of the pricier tools that can expand your author business. When you successfully master the strategies in this book, you should have the resources and the knowledge to invest effectively in your writing business if your goal *is* to quit your day job.

WHERE ARE YOU WITH YOUR WRITING CAREER?

If you have already written one or more books but you are struggling to get traction with sales, this book was written with you in mind. You may still be struggling to get paying readers. Maybe you're making fifty dollars a month, or three hundred, but you're barely breaking even on your editing, cover design, and proofreading investment.

I was in your position a few years ago, and this strategy helped me build an audience and ramp up my business to $1,000 a month. The strategy I outline to get your writing to $1,000 a month may require some changes to your books, your mindset, your marketing—or all three.

If you haven't finished writing your first novel yet, you may find this book helpful to map out the next books you plan to write so that they can be successfully marketed, then follow this strategy once the books have been written. (This book can also help writers of narrative non-fiction and memoir in addition to fiction authors, but it is not intended for authors of "hard non-fiction"—self-help, business, or biographies.)

WHAT CAN YOU EXPECT FROM THIS STRATEGY?

In order to achieve the two goals set forth above, this book will discuss how to create novels that maximize your chances so that once readers start them, they'll buy others you write. Once you have those books in your catalog, you can then get them in front of an interested audience—with proven tools that won't break the bank.

This book will **not** tell you how to make $1,000 a month from a **single** work of fiction. Most self-published authors don't have the resources to attract readers to their debut novel—there won't be any guidance on making you the next Paula Hawkins, Zadie Smith, or Donna Tartt. Those authors all had massive marketing machines behind their debut novels.

This book is also not a get-rich-quick scheme. Building a following for your writing takes multiple books—and it will take time. To maximize your chances for success, you'll need multiple novels, usually in the same series, in a reasonably popular genre, and (most importantly) fulfilling the expectations of those readers. If you have an existing series of books, this might only take months; if you don't, implementing this strategy could take much longer.

I'll discuss not only the places where you should invest your time, effort, and money in order to reach $1,000 a month, but also areas to avoid. I won't discuss a lot of the nuts and bolts about self-publishing, except when the inner workings of the process are relevant to getting to $1,000 a month—for example, the editing process, to make sure your book is as good as one from a major publisher. You won't get step-by-step instructions on how to upload EPUBs to retailers or how to design a book cover. You *will* get recommendations on what you should focus on, how to think about your books, and how to implement a marketing strategy to achieve your goals.

SUCCESSFUL AUTHOR BUSINESSES ARE SUCCESSFUL AT MARKETING

Most authors know that accounting and taxes need to be dealt with for any business to succeed—even independent author businesses. Similarly, authors must be able to market their books successfully in order to build audiences who'll buy their books, using as few resources as possible to get the word out.

This book will discuss some basic marketing concepts and how they apply to marketing your books—and yes, even when you're not yet making $1,000 a month, these concepts apply to you.

HOW MUCH SHOULD YOU EXPECT TO SPEND TO GET TO $1,000 A MONTH?

Author businesses don't have nearly as many startup expenses as other types of businesses. But when I started, I soon found out that certain things I needed to do came with a price tag.

One-time costs: book development

Although many writers don't think about the cost of developing a book, books require investment to create. While you may think that it only costs your time and effort (and maybe a laptop and writing software), other costs must be factored in if you're going to be successful, such as the following.

Tools: your laptop and software

This is very personal. Some people are fine writing with a $200 Chromebook and free Google Docs. Unfortunately for my wallet, I learned computing on the Mac platform (way back in the late 1980s), and I've used Microsoft Word since roughly the dawn of time. Even though I know there are better and cheaper alternatives, I'm so comfortable using Word on the Mac that I easily drop into a highly productive creative state that I find elusive on other platforms. So I write on a Mac using Word. Still other people find writing longhand in notebooks is how their muses most easily visit.

Listen to your muse, because you must get the words out of your head and onto the page. Whatever your preference, you must factor the cost of getting and using those muse-attracting tools into your business.

Logistics: ISBNs and barcodes

If you're going to self-publish books, you'll need ISBNs (International Standard Book Numbers). Most e-retailers won't let you sell an book without either submitting your own ISBN, or getting one from the e-retailer (Amazon is a notable exception for ebooks only, as it has its own ebook identification numbering system). You'll need a separate ISBN for each version of the book (e.g., one for the ebook, one for the paperback, one for the hardback, one for the audiobook). There is much debate on the advantages to purchasing your own ISBNs, or whether you can simply use the ones given away for free on most e-retailers (Amazon, Barnes & Noble, Apple Books, and others). Some print services require you to purchase your own (or purchase from the print service). In some countries, ISBNs are free. In the USA, ISBNs are fairly costly to purchase one at a time, but they are available in bulk with steep discounts. Likewise, barcodes are required on all print books, placed on the back cover. I've always been able to use free web tools to create barcodes.

Hired services

You will need to hire editors, proofreaders, cover designers, and interior layout specialists. Depending on the book formats you decide on (discussed in a future chapter), you may also require audiobook narration.

Hired services may be your biggest expense. It's possible to do some of this work yourself, but, as we'll discuss, it's not usually advisable—unless you have professional experience performing that service. Many of these per-book costs are necessary expenses in order to get a professional quality product created—and a professional product is almost always necessary to meet your readers' expectations and get your income to $1,000 a month. (Many first-time indie authors who don't have money to spend do at least some of these services themselves, or find an inexpensive alternative; while not recommended, sometimes it must be done out of necessity.)

Editing is my biggest expense. I hire three separate editors for various levels of style, quality, and polish. First, a developmental editor focuses on structure, character, and overall plot. Next, a copy/line editor analyzes sentence structure, passive voice, and consistency issues. Finally, a proofreader focuses on typos, punctuation errors, and grammatical errors.

Cover design can vary widely in cost as well. If you're just starting out, I would suggest that you strongly consider "pre-made" covers, which generally look quite professional and are available for a fraction of the cost of a custom cover. If you *do* hire a cover designer to make a custom cover, I would suggest that you don't pay for commissioned artwork; the cost can be incredibly high, and new authors may not realize how to design a book cover that sells. Furthermore, you don't want to spend thousands of dollars on artwork that misses the mark. You can get pre-made covers for less than $150, and custom cover design for $300 or less. Commissioned art (that looks professional) often costs thousands of dollars—and that's not where new authors should be spending their money.

Don't steal art or photos online to make your cover; not only is it unethical, but it's likely you'll get caught—which will be expensive. Also worth noting is that cover designers will often use "royalty-free" artwork, which you will not have exclusive rights to use; you might see the same photo or illustration on another cover, advertisement, or article (and that's okay). Even though exclusive artwork is quite expensive, I've seen authors get angry when their cover's royalty-free artwork shows up elsewhere.

Ongoing costs: marketing and promotion

There is no getting around it: you will need to spend *some* money on promoting your books. There are several inexpensive tools I definitely recommend for authors who are starting out. At the very least, you'll need an email tool for your mailing list (some are free for your first 500 or 1,000 subscribers), website hosting and building tools, and services to get your books into readers' hands. Web searches can find you many options for the first two, from MailerLite and Author.Email for mailing list tools to Wix, WordPress, and Squarespace for web hosting and building tools (and dozens more).

For getting the word out about your books, I recommend starting with an inexpensive service like StoryOrigin or BookFunnel ($150 a year or less), and, when you're ready, paid promo newsletter services that can cost $5, $20, $50, or more every time you promote your book.

I believe it's well within the realm of possibility to spend $200 a month or less in order to make a profit of $1,000 a month.

WHAT IF YOU DON'T HAVE ANY MONEY?

Your journey will look different if you don't have this money to invest in your author business. It will likely be a longer route and you may make more mistakes. However, it is possible to be successful. Chapter 15 details no-cost ideas for replacing many of these paid services.

WHY SHOULD YOU LISTEN TO ME?

I built a $1,000-a-month author business with five novels within two years of releasing my first book. I did it without a guidebook, and I learned what worked. But I also made a lot of mistakes along the way—mistakes that I'll share with you, so you know what *not* to do.

PART ONE
SATISFYING BOOKS

CHAPTER 1
THE PESKY SIX-YEAR-OLD

EVER SINCE I was six years old, I've considered myself a novelist.

I used to design my own book covers when I was in elementary school, and even at that young age I started to write novels—though I got only a few pages into each spy novel or action-adventure. But my inability to finish a story at that young age didn't stop me from planning multiple twelve-book series, complete with original art on the covers, gushing (and completely fake) reviews from *The New York Times*, and sales copy right out of movie trailers.

As I went through junior high and high school, I wrote enough short stories to fill a novel-sized book, mimicking the collections of short fiction from Raymond Carver. A friend and I curated a collection of short stories from similarly minded writers from my senior class, and then I majored in creative writing at the University of California at Santa Barbara. For my "senior thesis," I wrote 100 pages of a novel—a pompous story taking after the worst traits of my favorite authors, complete with too-clever tongue-in-cheek footnotes and invented histories of nonexistent artists. I wrote myself into a corner after my hero and heroine finally acted on their thinly-veiled attraction to each other—but by then, I'd hit page 100 and could turn my book in. (I can still picture my advisor skimming the first few pages and sighing in frustration.)

When I graduated, I tried to restart that bookstrosity in vain, but after a year or so, I put my creative energies into music. I played keyboards and wrote music for two semi-successful local pop/rock bands, and I got a day job in graphic design.

As my early twenties morphed into my mid-twenties, I worked on a short story every now and then—I even got published in a short fiction anthology filled with lots of other writers who took themselves too seriously.

But those short stories faded into the background, and that pretentious novel stayed in my bottom drawer. I got married to a fantastic woman, and I left the band and my dreams of music stardom when we were pregnant with our first child. My graphic design job became a decent technology marketing career...and I no longer focused on fiction.

One day, over a decade ago, I woke up, realized I was pushing 40—

And I'd never written a novel.

It didn't come as a shock to me that I hadn't written a

novel, but part of me was still that six-year-old kid who *knew* I'd be a novelist.

However, you can't exactly call yourself a novelist when you haven't finished a novel. Heck, I hadn't even *worked* on my novel in over a decade. I'd tried a few things in fits and starts, but I'd never gotten beyond thirty or forty pages of anything else.

As crushing as that realization was, I had another epiphany: I'd been trying to write what my university had told me to write: literary fiction—the pretentious metafiction that folded in on itself and prided itself on being more clever than everyone else in the room.

I liked *reading* literary fiction, but in a startling burst of clarity, I admitted to myself that I didn't like *writing* literary fiction.

What I liked *writing* was murder mysteries.

And that took me right back to my six-year-old self.

I was an early reader, and I consumed a ton of Encyclopedia Brown and Danny Dunn books in elementary school. In junior high school, I read dozens of Agatha Christie novels, along with *Two-Minute Mysteries*, Ngaio Marsh, and P.D. James.

Where had that kid gone? Where was the joy from figuring out the killer's identity? Where was the delight in watching the puzzle pieces come together just before the sleuth figured everything out? I'd spent the previous fifteen or twenty years with blinders on when it came to my writing.

At the time of my series of epiphanies, my wife was

considering going into nursing, and she started looking at careers. The week before, she'd looked up from her internet research and said, "Did you know that with a nursing degree, I could be a county coroner?"

That comment, along with my stunned realizations, planted the seed of an idea for a mystery novel into my head: A nurse who becomes a county coroner and solves murders.

With those epiphanies came a newfound dedication. I decided that I would participate in National Novel Writing Month—"NaNoWriMo" for short. (The concept of NaNoWriMo is simple: aspiring authors start new novels, and the goal is to write 50,000 words—about 200 pages—in the month of November.)

I posted my 50,000-word goal to Facebook. I came up with the first name of my heroine: Fenway. An odd first name for anyone, especially a woman, as it's the name of the stadium where the Boston Red Sox, a famous American baseball team, play their home games.

Who in their right mind would name their daughter Fenway? The answer came immediately: a selfish man who is more devoted to the Red Sox than to his family. My wife had given me Fenway's occupation: coroner. And with just those pieces, the identity of the murderer popped into my head.

With a vigor I hadn't had since college, I started writing furiously. Within ten minutes, I had 200 words, and then 200 more. I got 1,000 words written that first day—and I went to bed that night with thoughts of winning an Agatha award and hitting the bestseller lists.

And the next day, I wrote nothing.

And the day after that, I wrote nothing.

In the space of a week, that 50,000-word goal became, in my mind, unattainable.

Sure, I told myself that it was because I was working crazy hours for my company. I had to travel out of town a few times. And with Thanksgiving coming, and getting ready for Christmas, I must have been fooling myself to think I could write a novel in a month.

December came and went. And another December, and another one after that, and another.

Seven years after that first burst of 1,000 words—on October 30, 2017—Facebook helpfully served me up an "On This Day" announcement. It was a rehash of my confident declaration to the world that I would write a 50,000-word novel in November 2010. A stabbing reminder that it had been the better part of a decade since I had written a word about Fenway the Coroner and her estranged father.

Part of me felt like a failure. Part of me wanted to kill any hope I had left of writing a book.

But that stubborn six-year-old in my brain still insisted—more forcefully this time—that *I am a novelist*.

So on November 1, 2017, I started again.

As the famous quote says, "Insanity is doing the same thing over and over and expecting different results." I'd tried and failed to write a novel in four different decades. Something had to change.

So what would I do differently this time to make sure I wouldn't write the first couple of days and then give up?

I was in a different place in my life. I was in a less stressful job than I'd had in 2010. My kids were older and getting more independent. But though I had a goal, I wasn't sure I had the will to get to that goal. Before, I'd write a few pages, then go back every day and edit everything I had written up to that point. Sometimes it went further than that: I'd get so stuck on trying to fix what I'd written the day before that I couldn't write anything new. I'd fool myself into thinking I was still making progress if I'd edited a few pages even if I hadn't moved forward. Re-editing like this, day in and day out, had become the death of my pretentious senior thesis novel.

Could I break myself of that habit of rewriting my book to death? And if so, how?

I thought about this all the time. I wasn't sure how to keep myself motivated or keep myself going. I knew that when I reread the last sections I wrote, I was often doubting how good it was. Then I'd want to re-edit the sections I'd already edited. Then, one day in the car, after dropping my younger son at soccer practice, the answer came to me.

What if I told myself that no matter what, I would finish the novel?

I wouldn't edit or re-edit. I'd get myself into the flow by reading the last two or three paragraphs I'd written the previous day, but I would completely focus on writing new words.

I also promised myself I wouldn't spend more than a day away from writing. I don't think every successful writer needs to write every day, but I needed the discipline and the routine. The longer I was away from my novel, the less chance there was that I'd finish.

But none of that was more important than telling myself that I would write it until it was done. I promised myself this: even if I thought my novel was horrible, even if I thought it couldn't be saved, even if I thought it was a complete waste of time, I'd still write it until it was done.

I began in earnest on November 1, 2017. I wrote the entire first draft of *The Reluctant Coroner* in first person, from Fenway Stevenson's point of view (for those of you not familiar with the series, she's the title character and the sleuth in the mystery). One scene in an early chapter was emotionally excruciating to write, and I did stop writing for two days—but I came back through sheer force of will. And I kept making progress. NaNoWriMo's 50,000-word goal means writing an average of 1,667 words per day, and I was almost always exceeding that.

But about two-thirds of the way through my book—right around November 25—I read the paragraphs I had written the day before. And I frowned. Was Fenway coming across as whiny?

I read back a little further. Then a little further.

Oh no.

Fenway *was* whiny. She came across as entitled.

Even worse, she was difficult to like. How in the world could I have a successful novel with a character that no one would root for?

In years past, this would have prompted me to give up on the novel. But I remembered the promise I'd made: I would finish the book no matter what.

Then it dawned on me: Fenway was whiny because she was narrating the bad stuff that was happening to her because the book was in first person. When she was detailing her own thoughts and having issues with those around her, she sounded like she was complaining.

The answer was obvious: I would need to rewrite the book in third person, not first person.

Even though I had gotten my answer, the amount of work to convert it to third person would be vast. Plus, despite writing it in Microsoft Word, I couldn't do a global search-and-replace, because there is a ton of dialogue that has "I" and "my" and "we" and "me" that would be wrong if I changed it to "Fenway" and "Fenway's."

I didn't want to do all that work to make those changes. I wanted to give up. But that pesky promise—and that even peskier sixth-grader inside my head—made me realize that I *had* to finish the book.

So I did.

I was very close to my monthly goal of 50,000 words anyway—and after rededicating myself to finishing the book, I blazed past my goal. At the end of NaNoWriMo, I'd written 61,000 words, and I kept writing into December. Finally, on December 16, I typed "The End"—just past 83,000 words—and for the first time in my life, I had finished the draft of a novel.

Despite the work ahead of me on this Frankendraft, I had a sense of accomplishment that was different from anything else.

It wasn't ready for anyone else to read, and it needed a lot of work—maybe I wouldn't be up to the task of fixing it.

But I had finished writing a novel.

My inner six-year-old was delighted.

The experts say to put your finished first draft into a drawer for six weeks so you can read the book with fresh eyes. Yeah, well, that wasn't going to happen. The next day, I read the whole thing again to make sure my assessment was correct. Yes, for sure, it needed to change to third person. But there was, I felt, a solid story and a pretty good structure, and it was more than worth it to try to fix the novel.

My first edit was changing the first-person narrative to third-person. I rewrote phrases like "I rolled my eyes" to "Fenway rolled her eyes." I did one painstaking manual pass and changed probably two thousand instances of "I" and "me" and "my." Then another pass, where I discovered a couple of hundred instances of things like "Fenway rolled my eyes"—ugh. I also started to make some other changes: I fixed some continuity errors, I added more dialogue to a scene here or there, I streamlined scenes that were too wordy, and I added a couple of scenes that clarified Fenway's thought process during the investigation.

After putting a couple of hours in after work every day—and quite a bit on the weekends—in early January 2018, I had a novel that I considered… decent. Not great, but decent.

My inner six-year-old celebrated another major accomplishment. Not only was the book done, but it was pretty good.

For almost forty years, I'd considered myself a novelist, and now, *finally*, I had a finished novel. Yes, it took me about half my life to do it, but I'd done it. None of my friends had ever finished a novel. Even my fellow creative writing graduates from UCSB hadn't—a few had published short stories, but most were teaching English. *I'd written a novel.*

But now, a bigger question: What was I going to do with it?

CHAPTER 2
WHY I CHOSE TO SELF-PUBLISH

NOW THAT I HAD FINALLY—AFTER 40 years of stops and starts—finished my first novel, what would I do with it?

Was I going to put it in a drawer, never to be seen again? I immediately rejected that notion. It might not win a Pulitzer, but I wanted other people to read it. Not just that—I wanted other people to *buy* it.

I posted on Facebook that I had finished the book, and I got some congratulations, as well as a few people asking me the same question: what was I going to do with it? Some of them even asked if they could read it.

I was reading books long before the advent of e-readers. For most of my generation, getting an agent and having your agent find a publisher was simply the way authors got published. As I started researching the agent-and-publisher road, I began to get disheartened. The first step was to query agents, and that would take a year (or, more probably, much longer) for someone to agree to represent *The Reluctant Coroner*—if it happened at all. Then it might take another year or more for my agent to convince a publisher to take it on. I'd written the book when the #metoo movement was ramping up, and there were timely themes in the book—and some sections that might make readers uncomfortable. I didn't want the novel to feel dated as soon as it came out—and maybe the timeliness of it (or the themes themselves) would prevent agents or publishers from accepting it. But that was the reality: if I went down the agent-and-publisher route, I should expect at least two years of limbo—if anyone would publish it at all! Also, there was the possibility that a publisher would want me to change much of what I thought gave the book its power.

Then I got a response on that Facebook post that changed everything.

A friend from high school wrote a comment. She had written a book, self-published it, and was making some good sales from it. Did I want to pick her brain?

Her name is Michelle Damiani, and in the mid-2010s, she had taken her whole family—her husband and three school-aged kids—and moved from the East Coast of the USA to a tiny village in central Italy. She had blogged about it, then came back home and edited those blog posts into a novel-length book. And she had self-published it—and it was selling well. (It's a great read, too, along with the novels she's written since, all set in Italy.)

Michelle and I got to talking, and she told me everything she'd done to prepare herself for self-publishing, including consuming podcasts, writing guides, marketing guides, and so forth. She told me about the online self-publishing tools of the major book retailers and aggregators.

And she read my first Fenway Stevenson novel.

Her feedback was kind but honest. I had something there. It needed editing, but Michelle thought it could be put into publishable shape.

I started listening to a few self-publishing podcasts, and I thought: this is a way forward. This could be six months, not two years.

I spent hundreds of dollars on an editor—she was on the inexpensive side, but she had edited several novels that had been self-published. I knew a talented graphic designer who offered to do my cover in exchange for a good bottle of bourbon. I convinced my reader and writer friends to be early readers for me.

And then my daydreams started. I could be the next Paula Hawkins, and my debut novel would soar onto bestseller lists. I'd hit seven figures in sales for the next two or three years, and I'd put out a well-received novel every year or two.

In May 2018—only about six months after I wrote the first paragraph in my first draft—*The Reluctant Coroner* hit the shelves.

The first month, my friends and family snapped it up.

I was getting good (if surprised) reviews. "You know, I bought it because you're my friend, but it's actually good!" But it wasn't Paula Hawkins money—not anywhere close. A couple of hundred bucks in sales, which didn't even pay for a third of the editing costs.

The second month... oof. Less than half the sales of the first month. Even less the month after that.

You might recognize many aspects of your debut novel's journey in this story. *Field of Dreams* lied to you: there's no truth to the story of "if you build it, they will come." Books—especially in self-publishing—don't sell themselves.

This book will explain what I did, over the course of two years, to go from publishing that first book with disappointing sales to five books in the Fenway Stevenson series where I was selling over $1,000 a month—and turning a profit. It was slow, but it was steady. I didn't spend thousands of dollars on ads, either. Instead, I carefully invested in a few tools—and I made some difficult choices along the way and I shifted my mindset. It was excruciating to make some of those decisions, but I put myself in a position to succeed.

I've also made some disastrous decisions which resulted in a lot of wasted time and effort. I'll chronicle those, as well.

There is no one right way to be successful, but there are methods for putting yourself in the best position to succeed.

Mindset has a lot to do with success.

And no, it's not about a positive attitude or daily affirmations. It's a mindset about the way you treat your author business, with an attitude toward your novels that might be hard to shift into—especially if you've put years of blood, sweat, and tears into your books.

CHAPTER 3
SETTING YOUR EXPECTATIONS

WRITING a novel can be thrilling and scary. Many aspiring writers aren't sure they will be able to finish a novel, much less sell it. But once a writer has spent the blood, sweat, and tears finishing that novel—sometimes after years or even decades of struggle—the idea of goals creeps in.

"What is it, exactly, that I want to do with this novel now that I've written it?"

If you're reading this book, chances are you're in a similar place to me when I finished my first novel in January 2018. And you've probably come to the same conclusion: you want to get your book (or books) out into the world, you want people to buy them, and you want to make some money. You may still be deciding whether you want to go the traditional route with an agent and a publishing house, or whether you want to self-publish your books.

YOUR EXPECTATIONS TO GET TO $1,000 A MONTH

You might have seen dozens of book marketing guides out there. Many are written by successful authors. I've read a lot of them, and some of those guides' suggestions are actionable and useful.

Sometimes, though, experts talk about their experience as if it's the only way to be successful—and that's just not true. Every writer's journey to success is different.

The guidelines below won't be true for every writer; in fact, I doubt that your journey to success will follow every single one of these guidelines. However, I believe that by following all (or most) of them, you'll set yourself up in the best position to succeed. Sometimes, you'll succeed in spite of not following a guideline; in some cases, you may find that you succeed specifically because you *didn't* follow a guideline. And sometimes, you'll find that you aren't having success even though you followed all the guidelines. As in all businesses, there's an element of luck (both good and bad) in an author business. Sometimes you will be convinced that you have followed all the guidelines, but you really haven't. (We'll talk about a situation I found myself in like that.)

Nevertheless, as the great Edna Mode once said, "Luck favors the prepared."

Here are the guidelines I've discovered in my writing career that I believe will give you the best chance to succeed.

DON'T EXPECT OVERNIGHT SUCCESS

"If you really look closely, most overnight successes took a long time." —Steve Jobs

When you've spent eight years of your life writing a book, it can seem like publishing your book is the end of a long road. And in a sense, it is—but it's also the beginning of your author business. Companies that make headphones, for example, don't spend millions of dollars developing headphones, put them up for sale, then just sit back and watch the profits roll in. They invest more money in distribution channels and marketing. They often hire salespeople to sell to customers or to retail stores. There's often just as much work to sell the headphones as there is to make the headphones in the first place.

We love the story of an overnight success, but it's largely a myth. Jojo Moyes and Sophie Kinsella, both writers for whom the media crafted stories of overnight success, slogged for years with other novels before their breakout hits. Even E.L. James, with her *Fifty Shades of Grey* trilogy held up as the pinnacle of "overnight success" for indie authors, spent years writing her story on fan sites, building a community, and making adjustments to appeal to the widest audience possible.

KNOW YOUR GOALS

Writing is a creative endeavor, and most of the self-published authors I've met online and at conferences are introverts. Many of us have a great relationship with the written word and think we don't have a great relationship with other people. And getting your book out into the world often means dealing with other people.

So it's important to know what you want to get out of your writing. Do you want to "break even" financially? Do you want to make decent "gig money" on the side? Do you want to eventually quit your day job and write full-time?

Also, making money from your writing—whether it's $1,000 a month to start or eventually being able to quit your day job—is a much different goal than getting writing awards or getting on a bestseller list. Be clear with what your goal is, and make sure you're pursuing those efforts which will get you closer to your stated goals. Everything else is a distraction.

Some authors believe that winning awards and getting on bestseller lists, critics' lists, or best-of lists can provide power for your book to the various algorithms on book retailer sites. However, the retailers are constantly tweaking (and sometimes breaking) those algorithms, and in my experience, you can't rely on awards or lists to effectively sell more of your books—especially if they're awards and lists none of your readers have heard of.

There *is* an upside to awards and bestseller lists—it's

called "social proof," and it often provides readers who are on the fence with a reason to make the purchase. However, spending your time, effort, and money applying for awards or getting in author box sets to get on a bestseller list is usually not an efficient use of your time and effort, and—if your goal is $1,000 a month—often a waste of money. While I am a USA Today Bestselling Author, I landed on that list because of a promotion I did on my first box set (Books 1-3, at a sale price of 99¢) to get people to buy my second box set (Book 4-6, which I was selling at $9.99). My goal was the money, not the list—although the list is awesome, and I don't shy away from printing it on the covers of all my new books. So many of these "bestseller run" promotions end up costing the author hundreds of dollars and don't juice the sales of any of the author's other books.

YOUR AUTHOR BUSINESS IS A BUSINESS

Many small businesses are backed by third-party investors. Often, the entrepreneur isn't playing with their own money. And many small businesses need a lot of capital to become viable: they need a product, a marketplace, sales and marketing, and a host of other items.

Many authors go into writing expecting not to put any money into self-publishing. But authors need the same things as other businesses: a product, a marketplace, and a sales and marketing approach. Therefore, the bad news is that in order to get your book out into the world, you will also require capital. The good news? Your author business doesn't need nearly as much capital as other businesses.

Your products are your books, and writing the first draft of those books usually doesn't require you to spend any additional money—just an investment of time (and writing tools and software, as mentioned in the introduction). But after your first draft, if you are self-publishing, you will need to spend some money. You must purchase author services (editing, cover design services or elements, interior layout). Some authors can do their own editing, cover design, and so forth; I know some authors who are successful doing everything themselves, but they're definitely in the minority.

More good news: distributing to e-retailers (for example, Amazon, Kobo, Apple Books) and your marketplaces is generally free. E-retailers have their own web-based interfaces for uploading your book and cover, for setting prices, and for getting virtual shelf space. You pay the retailer a percentage of each sale for the right to do this (usually 30% or so, though depending on the retailer, your price point, and the country of sale it may be as low as 5% and as high as 65%). These percentages, too, are great compared to the low margins most companies have on physical items. If you have your own online store (where you can keep 95% of your royalties), you'll need to put in some money to set that up.

Sales and marketing, however, are different beasts. There are strategies out there to get your book in front of readers for free. Word of mouth is not only free, but the most effective marketing type; unfortunately, it's also the most difficult marketing type to take advantage of. It costs money to get the word out. From simple things like an author newsletter to third-party promotions to complex ad campaigns, you should expect to pay for this. You may not be paying a lot. Email services for your newsletter can be free for your first 500 to 2,000 subscribers, and there are promos you can take advantage of for $100 a year, or $5 per promo. Realistically, you can hit $1,000 a month in profit with an outlay of $200 or so a month—but remember, that's in addition to the money that you spend getting each book ready for publication.

CHAPTER 4
MEETING READER EXPECTATIONS

MANY WRITERS START with the goal of simply finishing a novel. Thousands of people think they can write a novel and never finish. If you've finished a novel, that's a tremendous accomplishment.

But if you want to sell that novel—and sell the others you write as well—you must make your books something that readers want to spend money on.

THE IMPORTANCE OF READERS' EXPECTATIONS

As book marketing expert Nick Thacker says, you can't successfully market a bad book. But what do experts mean by "a bad book"? I've seen plenty of books that I would consider poorly written that are on the bestseller charts. I've seen several books by indie authors that are successful that have scores of grammar and spelling errors, point-of-view problems, character inconsistencies, and other basic problems. These are what any English teacher would call a "bad book"—yet they're still selling. Why?

It's because these books, for all their problems, are meeting (and exceeding) their readers' expectations. I remember being asked if I was familiar with a popular action-adventure fiction series. I said yes. Did I like the series? I said, not really. How many of the twenty-plus books in the series had I read? I thought about it for a moment and realized I had read *all* of them. Even though it wasn't my favorite series, it was still meeting my expectations—and I kept buying them.

This is the most important guideline of all: **meet your readers' expectations**. Some authors are fiercely protective of their art, and they write complex books that can't be easily defined. This can be very bad for their author business and for sales, because readers may not have any idea what to expect from their book.

You must look at your books through your audience's eyes. You must care about the same things they do. Forget what you know about your book and approach the e-retailer page as if you're making the buying decision. Do you think readers will get what kind of book it is? Do you think the product description (often called a "blurb") will get people to click "buy"? Do you think the preview of the book—usually its opening chapters—are compelling enough to make a potential customer read on?

You will probably have to let go of some closely held beliefs about one or more of your books. And this leads to what I think is the biggest mindset change of all: **thinking like your reader**.

THINK LIKE YOUR READER

Thinking like your reader is probably the most important step to take for sales success.

When you sell or give away a book, you're making a deal with your reader. The reader is not just investing monetarily; they're also investing time and hope into you as an author. A short novel—50,000 words and about 200 pages—can take four or five hours to read. A crime fiction novel, like the ones I write, are often 80,000 to 90,000 words, or about 325 to 375 pages; on average, a good seven- or eight-hour investment.

When a reader is looking for something to read, they want something they think they'll enjoy. Figuring out what they'll enjoy next can be a time-consuming and sometimes painful experience for the reader. Maybe they will go to their e-retailer page of the last book they read—or the page that pops up on their e-reader after they're done with their last book—and they'll click on other book recommendations. Sometimes they'll go to their e-retailer site and search for their next book.

So—how will that reader find you?

And once they find you, how will they choose *your* book over the dozens of others that show up?

Authors who don't meet their readers' expectations

won't sell many books. And meeting reader expectations starts with writing the book itself.

HOW READERS FIND BOOKS

If you're like most readers, there has been a point in your recent past where you said to yourself, "I don't have anything to read." (Ignore, for the moment, the large pile of unread books on your nightstand.)

Finding a book to read is a chore. Sometimes you can be lucky and a friend recommends something that you think sounds good, or maybe your book club's next monthly selection is on your bookshelf or is only an e-reader click away, but too often, a search for a new book requires wandering around in a virtual bookstore looking for something you think you'll like.

Many people start with the genre they're interested in. They browse covers and click on the ones that look like the kind of book they'd like. Sometimes they'll search for a particular characteristic of a book. Sometimes they'll go through their emails, looking for the book newsletters they signed up for. This is a frustrating process for many readers, full of uncertainty over whether they'll actually like the book they select, possibly wasting five to ten hours of their lives on an unenjoyable book.

Readers want to reduce this uncertainty. When a reader finds an author they really enjoy, the question of what to read next is easily answered—and if the book is the first in a series, that's even more compelling.

Do you remember the glee you felt when you found an author you could stick with through a whole series or a whole catalog? It's not only delightful and exciting, but there's a palpable sense of relief that comes with it too. You don't have to wonder what book you're going to read next. You don't have to spend hours searching book recommendations or have that sense of dread that you might hate the book you get. Instead, you can be confident that the next book in the series will be something you like and something you want to read.

MAKING DECISIONS ABOUT THE BOOKS YOU WRITE

While writing is a form of art, the selling of books is a business. Businesses that sell software, toothpaste, or gadgets must decide what type of audience to pursue, how their products will be different from others on the market, and what benefits their products will give to customers. Authors need to make similar decisions in order to appeal to their buyers. Some of the most important decisions you will make about your book include:

- What genre or category will you write in?
- Will you write series or standalone books?
- Will you write short stories, novellas, full length novels, or a mix of two or three of them?

GENRE: CATEGORIZING YOUR BOOKS

If you're writing in a well-established category, you may already know what readers expect. In romance novels, there must be a "happily ever after" ending. In mystery novels, the sleuth must be the one to unmask the killer. There are many other more subtle reader expectations in various genres, but you know as a reader the level of disappointment you'd feel if you spent five hours reading a romance novel to have the heroine break up with her significant other at the end.

Authors don't always think about the expectations that readers will bring with them when they start the book. Often, authors who are just starting out will write the book they've always wanted to write—and feel that they are transcending the concept of genre. If their friends or families ask what type of book it is, or what the book is about, the author sometimes has trouble categorizing the book. It may have elements of several different genres—a little sci-fi, a little romance, a little fantasy, a little women's fiction.

The trouble with multi-category books? Marketing those books to potentially interested readers is difficult—and your readers may not expect what your multi-category book is doing. Authors are always asked, when they upload their books on e-retailer sites, to put their books into categories of genre and subgenre.

TARGETING THE RIGHT AUDIENCE: CHOOSING A PRIMARY GENRE

It's okay not to know at first. With my first novel, I didn't know either. But I did know that I thought my book was pretty close to Sue Grafton's Kinsey Milhone mysteries (*A is for Alibi* is the ultra-famous Book 1 in that series).

Discovering books similar to yours—like I did with the Kinsey Milhone series—is often called **finding your comps**, short for comparables. This is often the first step to marketing independently published books that experts will recommend. If you can find books similar to yours, then you can target the same audience.

Choosing your comps is tricky. You want to find books that are similar in tone, feel, and plot, but they don't have to be too similar. For example Grafton's books and my books both have strong female sleuths with an independent streak; both books are set in towns on the California coast; there's a splash of romance; there's a little sex and violence, but nothing explicit or gory; there are a few swear words, but not many. There are also a couple of differences: Grafton writes her Kinsey books in first person; Kinsey is a private investigator, not a coroner like mine; and Kinsey's relationship with her father isn't a plot point. There are plenty of commonalities that Grafton readers would like, even with the differences. Approach finding your comps in a similar manner: start with genre and tone, and move to setting and character. One author in one of my groups dismissed a comp because her book featured a heroine in the U.S. Army, and the comp had a heroine in the Air Force; that attitude will dismiss many helpful books that are actual comps.

In my case, I studied the book categories of Grafton's books. This gave me a very good idea what I should use for my genres and categories: the main genre is *mystery*, and the subgenres are *hard boiled*, *private investigator*, and *women sleuths*. (Be warned, though, that not all e-retailers use the same category names.)

While there are elements of police procedural, medical thriller, and even a dash of romance in *The Fenway Stevenson Mysteries*, the main genre I've picked for the books is "hard boiled," as I believe that my books align most closely with what hard boiled mystery readers expect.

Another reason to choose a genre is to figure out what marketing tactics successful authors have used with the audience you're targeting. You can study their covers, their book descriptions, and their ads (if you see some). But beware: you may find your comps, but the audience might not overlap with yours as much as you think. In my case, Sue Grafton was a good choice to help me select my genre and category, but a poor choice for audience targeting. Why? Because Grafton's books are so popular that targeting those audiences is very expensive—but worse than that, people who aren't usually fans of hard boiled mystery novels will read Sue Grafton. If you have a limited amount of money to spend on marketing, don't spend it chasing an audience that reads only one specific author in your genre. That means if you're a horror writer, you don't want to use Stephen King's audience, because a lot of his readers don't read any other horror writers. If you're a fantasy writer, don't target J.R.R. Tolkien.

Instead, you want to find books—preferably by other indie authors—who are popular within your genre, but not *too* popular. Finding authors like this is tricky. I found something that worked: the e-retailer pages for the Sue Grafton novels later in the series (the twentieth and twenty-first books in particular) often had a section further down the page with the subhead "books related to this item" or "readers also purchased." This section is often called the **also-boughts** by book marketing experts. The later books in the series tended to be read by more hard boiled fans, and these also-boughts were usually well-regarded novels by successful but less popular authors. It was this set of books that helped me figure out what types of covers, book descriptions, and audiences I should focus on.

GENRE MASH-UPS

N.K. Jemisin's *The Broken Earth Trilogy* is a combination of genres. *The Verge* called the trilogy a blend of "fantasy, science fiction, and post-apocalyptic tropes." But the category in which most booksellers place *The Broken Earth Trilogy* is "science fantasy." Similarly, Becky

Chambers' *Wayfarers* series combines elements of science fiction, action-adventure, and LGBTQ+. Most popularly, it's categorized as a "space opera."

If you have written a genre mash-up, it's important to figure out which categories to use to meet reader expectations, because those expectations will shape everything you do to market your book.

If you're in this situation, the best thing to do is to find your comps—in this case, books that have similar genre mash-ups and see what they've done. However, if your particular mash-up is unique, you won't be able to find similar books, which can be very frustrating.

Your editor(s) and early readers can sometimes help with this. If you ask them what genre they think it is, it's possible that they can identify the **primary genre**. Yes, your book might be part space opera, part LGBT romance, and part medical thriller, but if most of your early readers categorize it as a space opera, then you should market your book as a space opera. You may think you've written a hard-to-categorize mash-up of women's fiction, time travel, and murder mystery, and an experienced writer or several of your early readers might tell you that it's clearly more of a police procedural mystery than anything else.

Experienced indie authors might also have some valuable input—but only if they read or write in genres that are adjacent to what you're doing. If you have an epic fantasy/space opera mashup, don't ask a romance writer to give you categorization advice!

If you're asking early readers for their advice, I recommend not limiting your feedback to one or two readers. One piece of feedback is an anomaly; two might be coincidence. When you get similar feedback about a genre (or anything else—a passage in your book, a character, etc.) from more than two people, it's time to address the issue. If you suspect your book would be best characterized as magical realism, but three early readers think it's urban fantasy, I strongly suggest categorizing the book as urban fantasy.

GENRE: DECIDING WHETHER TO WRITE TO MARKET

For years, analyst firm K-lytics has reported that romance novels have sold the most units, followed by crime and mystery. There are dozens of subgenres in each category, however, and some of the subgenres sell much better than others.

That doesn't mean that you should choose to write in one of the most popular subgenres, though. Writing in a genre with which you're *extremely familiar* will be likely to result in you, as the author, meeting the readers' expectations—and often allows you to give just enough of a twist to make the book intriguing without going too far. That will maximize your chance of success and get you closer to that $1,000-a-month goal.

If you choose to write in a genre you're not as familiar with, you can miss some of the reader expectations or you can write a story that hews far too closely to clichés.

There are exceptions to all of this, of course; there are indie authors who have pretty much invented their own genres who are successful, but again, those are the exceptions. Many successful indie authors bombed in their early work because they wrote hard-to-categorize books that never found the right audience.

On a personal level, it's important to enjoy the writing that you do. Yes, it can feel like work, but it shouldn't feel like a slog. Many authors who slog their way through writing a book will create characters that aren't compelling, a plot that drags along, and themes that don't resonate with the audience. In other words, a book that's a slog to write will result in a narrative that is just as much of a slog to read.

But authors can take that too far in the other direction: they can write books mashing up genres they enjoy, or a book that breaks the expected conventions of the genre so much that no one wants to buy it. (Later, I will discuss my romance books, which were a fiasco, even though I really enjoyed writing them.)

That's why every writer's journey is different. Some authors can purposely write in popular genres using popular tropes and do very well; others will produce works that are clichéd and derivative (and don't sell). Many successful authors strike a balance between what they love writing and what will sell, but where the pendulum swings in your author career will be unique to you.

GENRE: MAKE SURE READERS KNOW WHAT TO EXPECT

Several authors I know have written books that don't fit neatly into a single genre or subgenre, and generally speaking, those books struggle with sales. Their books can be (and often are) masterful, but if readers don't clearly understand what type of experience they'll have with the book, they'll move on to something else.

TITLES, COVERS, AND DESCRIPTIONS

Your book and series titles, your book covers, and the descriptions (often called **blurbs**) of your books are sometimes considered part of the book itself and sometimes considered part of the marketing of the book. However they're categorized, these are very important toward establishing your audience's expectations. An action-adventure novel titled *Passion in the Forest* isn't going to set reader expectations properly. By the same token, a romance novel with a cover that looks like a self-help book will only serve to confuse your audience. And a book description that is light on intrigue and heavy on plot details will have your readers snoozing before they can click the Buy button.

Your self-published manuscript must be indistinguishable from a traditionally published book—and that goes for the whole package: title, cover, and blurb. There are whole books dedicated to these items, many of which are quite good, and I discuss covers and blurbs later in this book.

I recommend listening to specific episodes of a podcast called *The Self-Publishing Show* (formerly *The Self-Publishing Formula*) called "BookLab." In these episodes, three book experts look at the cover, the blurb, and the first few pages of self-published novels to see where they can better match reader expectations. I suggest you follow along with the supplied PDFs that you can download from the show's website so you can see the before-and-after transformation of the books.

SERIES OR STANDALONE?

Some authors don't like to read series and don't like to write in series. They'll point to some of the most successful authors out there, like Stephen King, and point out that they primarily write standalone novels.

As an indie author, however, your chances of getting readers to follow you from book to book will increase dramatically with series. Readers want to read books they like, and if they like Book 1 in your series, it becomes an easy decision what to buy and read next. Readers who pick up a standalone book and like it now have a decision when they look at the rest of your book titles. You would rather they don't get consumed with indecision and move to a different author. Having a next book in the series makes the decision much easier for them.

It's also much easier to make common indie author

marketing tactics work for you when you have a series of books. There are exceptions, but the vast majority of successful indie fiction authors write books in series.

One common question I've heard in many author marketing sessions is: "Do I have to write in a series?" The short answer, if you're looking to make money, is "probably." Simply put, if you have a successful series, the easiest way to make more money is to write another book in the series, because the marketing work has already mostly been done.

A **series** can be defined in many different ways. Many fantasy series have a long, **overarching arc** (a subplot that continues through multiple books) that is the fulfillment of a massive quest. Some adventure and mystery series also have overarching arcs—they have an episodic plot that begins and ends in each book, but there might be personal growth or interpersonal drama that showcases either a larger plot or a character changing from the beginning of the series to the end. These books almost always should be read in the order of the series.

Other series may have the same lead character who doesn't change significantly from book to book, and each book in the series does not have to be read in order. In many romance series, each book focuses on a different couple, but the series might revolve around a specific location, a group of friends, or a workplace. Becky Chambers' *Wayfarers* series focuses on different main characters in each book, but all of them are interconnected.

THE POWER OF A SERIES

In order to ensure that your readers know what book to read next, most indie author marketing experts recommend writing books in series—even if they're only loosely related. When a reader of Book 1 in a series goes on to buy Book 2, that makes the author money—and it's the concept most successful indie authors rely on to sell significant numbers of books.

This concept is known as **readthrough**: simply put, the percentage of readers who go on to read (usually by purchasing) the next book that the author wants them to read. If you have a series, you want the reader to finish Book 1 and buy Book 2, then Book 3 and so forth. If you have standalone books, it's more difficult for readers to know the next book they should read.

You see this with successful authors all the time: Sue Grafton published 25 Kinsey Milhone mysteries; Lee Child published more than 20 Jack Reacher books—and neither of them bothered publishing anything else. They didn't need to; once a reader gets hooked, there's a very good chance they'll purchase many books in the series.

When we're done with one series from an author, the easiest place to go is to another series by that author in the same genre. Authors can expect to see some drop-off between series, but quite often the second or third series becomes even more successful than the first (Suzanne Collins springs to mind as an example: her *Hunger Games* trilogy was much more popular than her still-successful *Gregor the Overlander* series, which was published earlier). When this happens, too, it can bump up the sales of your **backlist**—books that you haven't published recently but that are still in your catalog.

I've heard from both readers and authors who *don't* like to read novels in series. They may prefer authors who write standalone books. That's fine if you prefer reading that way, but as an author, know that it's much easier to convince a reader to buy the next book in your series than it is to ask them to choose from your list of standalone novels.

If you *do* write standalone novels, it's a much steeper hill to climb. You will need to follow many of the suggestions for books in series, and it helps if you have books set in the same universe or with the same characters. At the very least, you can cross-promote books in the same genre with the same tropes.

BOOK OR STORY LENGTH

Traditionally, young writers are encouraged to sell their short stories to periodicals (which are now few and far between—especially the ones that pay). Shorter books—novellas that are 20,000-50,000 words—can sell, particularly if they're part of a fast-paced series. (A.C. Fuller, for example, has a successful novella series called *The Crime Beat*.)

However, most readers like to sink their teeth into full novels; readers *expect* full-length novels. Although lovers of satirical comedies, steamy romance, and science fiction have a higher tolerance for short fiction compared to readers of mysteries and epic fantasy, full novels sell much better than novellas or short story collections. Full novels are often required for many of the promotions we'll discuss in later chapters (though, as always, there are exceptions).

You'll maximize your chances for sales with full-length novels because you'll be meeting reader expectations. (You'll also generally be able to sell full-length novels for more than novellas; we'll discuss pricing in a later chapter.)

And what happens when you don't meet your reader expectations? Unfortunately for me (but fortunately for you), I know firsthand what that's like—and I know a few ways to address the problem.

CHAPTER 5
MY EXPERIENCE WITH READER EXPECTATIONS IN MY BOOKS

I KNOW the issue of meeting—and failing to meet—reader expectations with my writing. I've failed three times by not thinking like my readers and not meeting their expectations.

SUCCESS: THE FENWAY STEVENSON MYSTERIES

I mentioned in the first chapter how I've loved mysteries ever since I was a kid. Although my debut novel was a little slow to start and a little rough around the edges, it nevertheless provided me a good foundation. My books were clearly similar to Sue Grafton's Kinsey Milhone mysteries, so I knew that if I could get in front of an audience like that, I'd have a better chance of success.

This book series met the expectations of readers of similar books, and I was able to find effective ways to get in front of these audiences, using the marketing techniques defined in this book. A high percentage of readers who start this series buy most of the books, leading to the majority of my sales—and driving almost all the business to my early goal of $1,000 a month.

FAILURE: BAD WEATHER

After writing my third book in the Fenway Stevenson series, before I started on book four, I discovered an old short story I'd written in college. Originally, *Palm Sunday*, set in 1992 (when I wrote it) was about a man who confronted a female identity thief (and possible romantic partner). The story was in the genre of "literary fiction," but I liked it a lot.

In the Fenway Stevenson mysteries, the title character works with a female sergeant in her early 50s, Dez Roubideaux, who's snarky, outspoken, and gay. I got great feedback on Dez—many people said that she was their favorite character.

I had an idea for *Palm Sunday*: I decided to put Dez back in 1992, when she was getting her bachelor's degree in criminology, and substituted her into the main character's role. I toned down the religious imagery and the philosophical nature of the plot, then changed the name *Palm Sunday* to *Bad Weather* (which was the original name for my short story). I bumped up the romantic elements, I made the identity theft the main plot, and it grew from a thirty-page short story to a 175-page novella.

My editor thought it was quirky but interesting. He had an idea about how to smooth down the edges of the quirkiness to make it more cohesive—but that would have required a lot of rewriting, and I was keen to get onto Fenway 4. So my editor and I compromised (you can do this as a self-published author, after all) and I addressed a few of the worst issues and went through the rest of the self-publishing process.

Bad Weather was released a few months after Fenway 3, which until that point was my most successful book, anchoring my $300-a-month sales. I had visions of all my readers flocking to see a young Dez pre-academy, and loving this quirky identity-theft-and-LGBT-romance novella.

Instead, *Bad Weather* tanked—and to this day it's my worst-reviewed book. People didn't know what kind of book it was: they were expecting a Fenway Stevenson mystery with Dez as the sleuth, and instead, they got a college student fumbling her way through a romance with a sketchy partner. Looking back, it's unsurprising that my readers reacted so negatively.

It's not that *Bad Weather* is a bad book. It's still quirky, and it raises some interesting philosophical questions without getting preachy. But it's not the book my readers wanted. People who read all the Fenway Stevenson books will still sometimes buy *Bad Weather*, but it doesn't sell very well.

I sure didn't learn from that experience, though, because after I published Fenway 4, I then decided to write a series of romance books with a twist.

FIASCO: THE ROMANCE BOOKS

I had a few friends who were romance novelists, and I'd been an early reader for a couple of their books. I liked them, and after writing my fourth Fenway book, I needed a bit of a creative palate-cleanser. I thought I'd try my hand at writing a romance novel—or maybe a romance novel series.

I had a twist that I thought was brilliant: the couple at the center of each book would be married, but for all kinds of reasons had lost the romantic spark. The books would cover not only how they found their romantic spark again, but would flash back to how they originally got together.

Some of my romance author friends encouraged me to focus on this series instead of my Fenway series. They told me it would address an underserved market—wives who wanted more romance from their marriages. If I followed the romance structure and the genre conventions, they convinced me I could have a huge hit on my hands.

I wrote the books quickly—much faster than I wrote the Fenway books. First of all, the three volumes in the series were shorter—50,000 to 60,000 words instead of the 90,000 to 110,000 words of the Fenway books. (That length is good: romance readers generally expect novels in the 50,000-60,000 range.) But I also wrote many more words every day; often 3,000 or 4,000 words a day, compared to about 2,000 a day with my Fenway series.

I gave them to other romance authors and readers for feedback. One or two readers had some minor structural suggestions, but the books were generally very well received. I hired a professional romance editor, and got positive feedback. I hired a professional romance cover artist, and got three covers I thought were perfect.

I decided to **rapid-release** them (that is, release them within a month of each preceding release) under a pen name, and in the space of three months, I published all three books. Following the marketing advice I'll discuss later in this book, I gave away the first one for free on a couple of promo sites and soon had 10,000 downloads of Book 1 (and, using the techniques mentioned in this book, built a newsletter list of 2,000 subscribers for my new pen name). The first week, I got about 10 five-star reviews. It wasn't as many reviews as I hoped, but the reviews were effusive with praise.

I thought that duplicating what was successful with the Fenway series would give me at least a couple of hundred extra sales every month—at the very least. If my author friends were right and this series would scratch the itch of an underserved community, maybe I *would* have a massive hit on my hands.

I couldn't have been more wrong.

Usually, authors can expect a free Book 1 (often called a **free first-in-series**, or FFIS) to convert to three to five percent in sales to book two. Those 10,000 giveaways should have resulted in at least 300 sales of book two. Instead, I got 15 sales of book two. (That's not a typo: *fifteen* sales.)

I was incredibly confused. I thought the books were well-written. I thought I'd followed the "rules" of romance writing that I'd discovered: there was a "happily-ever-after" ending, and I thought the "heat level" of the romance was clear. I had an on-target cover and description. What was wrong?

I'm a member of a lot of Facebook writing groups, and one of them was offering a "Why isn't my book selling?" feedback service. So I applied to that service with my romance novels, explained what I did, what my goals were, and why I was confused.

The responses were almost immediate. Yes, the books were well-written. Yes, the covers were great.

The problem?

In most romance novels, the end goal is the wedding. I was starting with the couple already married.

So... my audience, who all wanted to read about a sweep-you-off-your-feet romance, had no desire to **start** a romance where the readers' expectation of the conclusion was already there. And they *really* had no desire to read the first couple of chapters about work and home and kids and family pressures.

When "forced" to read the books—that is, my early readers who had agreed to give me feedback—they loved the book once they got into it, especially as the stakes got higher and the couple rekindling their love became more evident. But no romance reader who saw the premise, the cover, and the blurb wanted to read it.

This wasn't just bad—it was potentially a devastating blow to the series and possibly even to my pen name. The entire premise of the series was massively flawed—it was doomed before it even got out of the gate.

It's worth noting that there are some successful romance novels where the couple is already married, but my books didn't successfully follow the tropes that would have met my readers' expectations. The series also didn't follow the tropes of the "second chance romance" subgenre, in which former lovers reconnect after a break-up and finally find their happy ending—because there was no break-up in my books.

The only question left was: Could the series be saved?

I've thought about this long and hard, and I think, hypothetically, I *could* rewrite the series so that it would meet the expectations of romance readers. There are some commonalities in each book and each relationship. The series could be rewritten to move all the action to the early stages of their relationships, pre-wedding, and the series could focus on those commonalities. It would require some extensive rewriting, but it could be done. In addition to the rewriting, I believe it would also need a new series title, new book titles, and probably a new pen name—all of which are a lot of work to change. But it could be done.

Why haven't I done the work to change these books?

Because of two unanswered questions.

First: The series could be rewritten, but was I the one to rewrite it? Could I give the rewritten books the correct touch in order to turn the series into a success? I liked romance novels, but I'd been reading the genre for less than a year. Even if I rewrote the series, do I know for sure that I won't leave out *another* aspect of romance reader expectations?

Second: Would it be worth it? I'd already sunk over $2,000 into professional editing, cover design, website design and hosting for a second pen name... and sold fewer than 50 books in the whole series. I'd need at least that much to redo the books, and I didn't have the confidence that I could recoup the additional cost.

There are several lessons that I took from the failure of my romance novels:

1. **Be cognizant about what your readers will expect**. I believe I did everything right in terms of marketing and sales. I wrote three books that reviewers and early readers loved. But the whole premise of the series failed to meet the expectations of my core audience because each book started with an already-married couple. I thought I was meeting reader expectations when I was badly missing the mark—and if I'd researched more carefully when writing a genre I didn't know very well, I might have figured this out

before wasting time, effort, and money. A corollary to this lesson is akin to the old writing adage "write what you know": if you don't know the expectations and acceptable tropes of a genre or subgenre, either immerse yourself in the genre and learn everything you can, or don't write in that genre. It was folly for me to attempt a series in this genre when I was a relatively new romance reader.

2. **Past performance is no guarantee of future success**. Americans hear this all the time on advertisements for investments—it's the same with books and book series. Very few authors can plug-and-play a second series or rest on their laurels. Each book and each series will take care and effort to meet reader expectations and be successful.

3. **Make changes when they make sense, but know when to cut your losses**. You may come to a point where you realize you need to make significant changes to the book itself in order for it to sell better. But if those changes are too extensive, or if you don't feel you have the talent or patience to make the changes that need to be made, stop promoting the books. Some authors feel like they need to remove them from the e-retailers. My romance books are still for sale (although they don't sell many copies), but

the website of the pen name author, the mailing list, and the promotions I ran are no more.

SAVING A FAILURE: MURDERS OF SUBSTANCE

So with a couple of failures under my belt, I turned my attention back to *The Fenway Stevenson Mysteries*. I wrote the fifth, sixth, and seventh Fenway books, then decided to write another murder mystery series. Because mystery is the genre I'm most familiar with and the one I've had success in, it's the genre I thought I could get a second successful series in. And I had a few ideas—but one of them really jumped out at me.

I'm a Gen-Xer who came of age in the eighties, and I loved the electronic music that defined a lot of the pop and alternative music of that decade. New Order was one of the most influential bands of the 1980s, growing out of the band Joy Division. They pushed the bounds of technology, sequencing, and tape loops. "Blue Monday" was without question the most influential dance track of the early 1980s, and songs like "Bizarre Love Triangle" and "True Faith" were big hits, especially on the alternative radio stations I listened to growing up.

I was listening to their 1987 compilation album, *Substance*, when I was struck with the thought that most of the songs on the album, from "Ceremony" to "Shellshock" to "Blue Monday" to "Bizarre Love Triangle," would make solid titles for murder mystery books.

As I turned this over in my mind, the name of the album itself—*Substance*—led me to the crux of the series: the homicide division of a fictional federal agency that focused on controlled substances. *Murders of Substance* was born—and with it, not only twelve book titles, but twelve matching book covers, all based on Peter Saville's iconic design of the *Substance* album cover.

My nerdy brain totally loved the idea. And the four lead characters in the books would all be based on the four band members, all cheekily named after the real band members!

The first main character was Dr. Kep Woodhead. He was named after New Order's bassist, Peter Hook, who is perhaps the most recognizable member and most responsible for its signature sound. Hook's given name is Peter Woodhead, and "Kepa" is Aramaic for "Peter."

The second main character is Bernadette Becker, the federal agent responsible for being Kep's handler. Her name is based on the lead singer and guitarist's name, Bernard Sumner ("beckoner" is a synonym for "summoner"). The other two characters' names are based on New Order's drummer and keyboardist.

I released *Ceremony* (track one on the *Substance* album has the same name) to much fanfare but disappointing sales. Even putting it on a 99¢ sale didn't goose the sales like I wanted. I figured I'd need to release a couple more in the series before it gained traction, so I quickly wrote *Everything's Gone Green* (the title has the same name as track two on New Order's *Substance*). I think this book might be one of the best I've written—but releasing that book didn't help much.

Once again, I wasn't thinking like my reader. My average reader may have been alive in the 1980s, but they weren't listening to New Order—and even if they were, they wouldn't be familiar enough with the band member names or the cover art to "get" any of the references I was making. (And even if they did, there was no connection between the New Order references and the murder mystery.)

The cover art, while gorgeous and a great homage to Peter Saville, looked more like a non-fiction book. It didn't look like any murder mystery book cover, and no one got the visual reference. This must have hurt sales of the book.

I loved Peter Saville's cover art, but I made the painful decision to get the cover art redone. I kept some of the original artwork concepts: a needle for Book 1 (*Ceremony*), and a gas mask for book two (*Everything's Gone Green*). The book covers, again, were gorgeous, and this time they looked like fiction books—thrillers, even!

But after the new book covers came out, they *still* weren't selling.

I asked a couple of book marketing experts why they might not be successful, and they were honest. Once again, I wasn't thinking like my reader—a needle and gas mask might have figured prominently in the stories, but that imagery made the books look like post-apocalyptic thrillers, not hardboiled whodunits—not helped by the titles of the books, either. It wasn't enough to look like a fiction book—the covers had to be on-genre.

Even the name of the series, *Murders of Substance*,

didn't meet audience expectations. Almost all successful mystery book series have the name of the sleuth (or the name of the location) in the title.

My editor and several of my early readers pointed all of this out to me, both when I was writing the first book and when I was getting it ready for release. But I couldn't be swayed: I was in love with the whole concept of the *Substance* album, and I thought I was very, very clever. One of my early readers said that the title of the second book (*Everything's Gone Green*) didn't work for her, but again, I was stubborn. From my perspective, the book *had* to be named *Everything's Gone Green* because the second track on the *Substance* album was "Everything's Gone Green." Now I realize how idiotic that sounds.

Put a different way: I was making the books about myself. The books were about what I liked, what I thought was clever, and everything that I prioritized. We often hear artists, writers, and musicians say that once they release their art into the world, it's no longer theirs—it belongs to the audience. I had forgotten that. I made *Murders of Substance* all about me—and my readers weren't interested.

The only thing that changed my mind was the sales—or rather, the lack thereof. I had to go through another even more painful process of renaming the series (using the sleuths' names, *The Woodhead & Becker Mysteries*), paying my cover artist to change the covers of the books (again!), and retitling the books. *Ceremony* became *The Winterstone Murder*, and *Everything's Gone Green* became *The Bridegroom Murder*. I also changed the lettering of my author name to match the Fenway Stevenson series covers, upon the advice of Erin Wright, who runs the Wide for the Win author group.

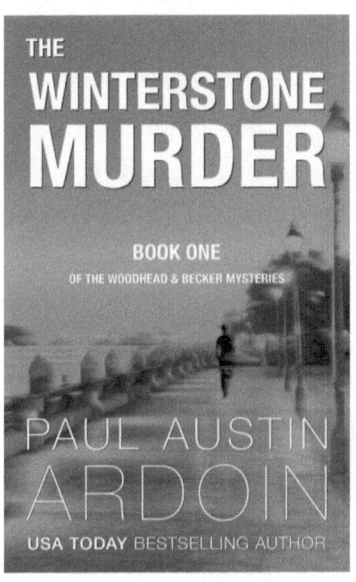

The New Order references in the book are still there—I didn't change the character names or anything else about the manuscripts themselves—but going forward, I won't worry about references to '80s post-punk electronica bands. Sales have gone up about 50% in the series—not as much as I wanted, but a big improvement from before. Had I launched the series correctly—thinking like my readers—to begin with, I might have had better sales at launch.

MY FAILURES IN PERSPECTIVE

With *Bad Weather* and my romance books, my failure to meet reader expectations can be traced to the *entire premise* of the novels. A genre is a promise, and those books didn't deliver.

In the case of *Bad Weather*, the disconnect with my readers was due to the content of the novel. With the romance novels, the book description revealed that the couple was already married and having problems—so no one even tried reading it. (As one of my romance reader friends put it, "I just read the blurb and I'm already exhausted." And not in a good way.)

With *Murders of Substance,* the cover art, the series title, and the book titles are what made mystery readers think they weren't going to get a murder mystery novel.

The Fenway Stevenson Mysteries, on the other hand, have delivered on their promises to the readers. The cover art and descriptions look and sound like the kind of mystery novel a Sue Grafton fan might like. The stories follow expected genre conventions while delivering on the structure and surprises of a hardboiled whodunit.

I hope you learn from my mistakes: in order to get to $1,000 a month, you need to think like your readers. When you don't, make the necessary changes to fix the problems—and if you can't, cut your losses and focus on your strengths.

CHAPTER 6
GETTING YOUR MANUSCRIPT READY TO PUBLISH

ONE OF THE big differences between traditional publishing and self-publishing is that you, as the author, are responsible for getting the book ready to publish once you've completed your manuscript.

In order to successfully sell your self-published fiction, most experts say that your book must look and feel indistinguishable from a traditionally published book.

The "look" part of the "look and feel" is, in my opinion, part of the marketing of the book—and we'll discuss marketing in later chapters.

But the "feel" of the book is about editing.

WHAT DOES EDITING ENTAIL?

Once you are happy with your draft manuscript, I recommend following a specific process to make sure your book is indistinguishable from one published by one of the big-name publishing houses.

ONE: THE SELF-EDIT

Experts will often tell you to put your book in a drawer for four to six weeks after you finish the first draft so you can look at it with fresh eyes. I've never been able to do this—I'm lucky if I can get through four to six *days* before I start self-editing.

One of the common questions I hear is, "How do I start self-editing?"

It depends on each author—self-editing is as personal as writing—but I can tell you what works for me.

Sometimes, I will have a pretty good idea of what the issues are when I start reading through the book. I write in Microsoft Word, and I will turn on "Track Changes" in the Review tab. If I'm feeling tentative, I'll start by correcting simple things, like typos or duplicate words. Then I will add comments when something doesn't make sense, or when I feel that something could be improved by a major change. As a mystery writer, I try to be aware of what I call "breadcrumbs"—small, subtle clues early in the story that, when a clever reader pieces them together, reveals the identity of the killer. I often don't have enough breadcrumbs early in the story, but when I read through, I can see where to add more breadcrumbs.

Sometimes it becomes clear that certain significant plot points aren't working, or there are major structural changes that need to be made. When this happens, I will often simply begin a rewrite from that point forward. It can be daunting, but often I can get the story back on track with a rewritten chapter or two (and smaller edits throughout) rather than throwing everything out and starting over.

It usually takes between three and five readthroughs before I'm satisfied with my manuscript—and I recommend stopping when you feel your book is of good (not perfect) quality. Often, authors (particularly early in their careers) can fiddle with manuscripts for months or years, delaying their progress and their publishing timeline. Keep in mind the proverb "Perfect is the enemy of the good." Authors who strive for perfection are in reality their own worst enemy. They're so busy trying to make their manuscripts perfect, they don't realize that finishing the book makes a much bigger difference than perfecting it.

TWO: ALPHA READER

The next step is finding one to three "alpha readers." These are people well-acquainted with your genre—you want someone who knows what readers of the genre expect. Don't choose a romance reader for your space opera or a fantasy reader for your spy thriller. Their expectations might be wildly different than your target audience, and they might give you ineffective feedback. You can sometimes find good candidates for alpha readers in your writing groups; I've found more alpha readers in writing groups that are online rather than in-person.

THREE: DEVELOPMENTAL EDIT

A developmental editor will look at the structure, plot, theme, characters, and other "big picture" issues in your manuscript. If there are any problems with the major elements of your story, this is the editor who will catch them. If you're just starting out, especially if you're at all unfamiliar with the genre, experts highly recommend this type of edit. Many developmental editors will offer a "trial" of a chapter or two at low or no cost, and many also will provide a second less comprehensive readthrough after you've fixed the first round of edits.

This type of editor will cost money. Depending on their level of experience and the length of your book, they can cost anywhere from a few hundred to a few thousand dollars.

I have had the same developmental editor for all my mystery novels since the second book I published: Max Christian Hansen. He can be harsh, but he is (irritatingly) usually right. He wasn't the first editor I worked with, but I believe his insights, questions, and problem identification have made every book he's edited better. Having the same editor has also given me consistency from book to book, which contributes to meeting reader expectations.

I suggest you do everything you can to see the value in the criticism of your work, whether the critique is given by an editor, proofreader, or early reader. Authors, like many creative people, tend to take criticism personally. Your ego can make it very difficult to fix a book so that it meets reader expectations, but you'll want to do everything you can to suppress your ego. After all, wouldn't you prefer that your editor point out problems now rather than a bunch of Amazon two-star reviews pointing them out after the book is published?

FOUR: BETA READERS AND SENSITIVITY READER

Once you've corrected everything the developmental editor has identified, find five to ten people who are fairly well acquainted with your genre to read the latest version. These people don't have to be as familiar with the genre as your alpha readers, but you do want them to be able to provide solid advice.

If one beta reader brings up an issue that you don't think is a problem, feel free to ignore it. If two or more readers bump on the same section or bring up the same issue, you will need to address it. However, focus on the fact that the reader identified a problem with your manuscript—not necessarily what the problem is or how to fix it. In my experience, readers often misdiagnose what the problem is or sometimes suggest a fix that won't work. It's up to you (or an expert editor) to get the diagnosis—and the remediation—right.

At this point in my process, I also hire a sensitivity reader to make sure I didn't put anything in the book that is insulting, sexist, racist, or otherwise problematic. If you choose to go this route, don't be defensive with what the sensitivity reader finds; we all have preconceived notions and long-standing biases that we aren't even aware of. My sensitivity reader has caught many things that would have embarrassed me if they'd been published, and I'm quite grateful to have this.

FIVE: LINE/COPY EDIT

After you address beta readers' issues, you're ready for a line/copy edit. Experts recommend getting a different person to perform this edit than your developmental editor. The line/copy editor focuses on point of view, consistency, passive voice construction, and so forth: not only grammatical items but story items that stick out. These editors often charge half-a-cent to one cent per word.

SIX: PROOFREAD

Once the line and copy edits have been made, hire a proofreader to fix punctuation errors, typos, and other fiddly mistakes (missing closed quotes are a big one). Many proofreaders charge less than half a cent per word, but again, it depends on experience.

SEVEN: READ IT OUT LOUD

No matter how many times you read your manuscript and no matter how many people you pay to edit and proofread, errors will get through. Reading the manuscript out loud will catch many errors that your eyes alone will miss. I've always found twenty or more errors when doing an out-loud reading.

CHAPTER 7
THE COST OF RUNNING YOUR AUTHOR BUSINESS

IF YOU WANT to make $1,000 a month as an author, your goal should be to attain that number *after* all your expenses are factored in. If you're getting $1,000 in revenue but spending $600 a month, you're only getting a net profit of $400 a month.

As mentioned earlier, your author business is a real business, even if you're the only "employee" and you're only spending a few hours a week on it. As with any business, your author business has startup costs—far lower than most other kinds of businesses, but nevertheless these expenses must be planned for.

Like many writers, I'm allergic to math and spreadsheets, but money is important. As much as it pains me to write this, planning and tracking your income and expenses is critical to reaching your financial goals.

Find a good profit-and-loss spreadsheet; templates are available online specifically tailored for indie authors.

To start your business, you will have some one-time

costs, and some recurring costs. Keeping track of these items will not only help you meet your goals, but in many countries (like the U.S.), you can—and should—claim your expenses as tax deductions. A quick web search of profit-and-loss sheets and one-time and recurring expenses will help you discover resources to assist you.

THE COST OF CREATING YOUR DRAFT

Writing the first draft of your manuscript usually requires a computer and writing software. Yes, you can draft longhand in notebooks or use a typewriter, but if you want to sell it, that book will need to turn into digital data. Fortunately, the bare necessities are cheap: you can purchase a Chromebook or an inexpensive Windows PC for less than $500 (a one-time cost), and there are free web-based word processing tools like Google Docs and LibreOffice. More robust writing tools like Scrivener or Microsoft Word cost money, and sometimes require a subscription. You'll also need a place to write, so if you decide to spend money on a desk, monitor, or chair, factor that into your costs (and remember to deduct those expenses from your taxes, if applicable).

THE COST OF YOUR FINAL MANUSCRIPT

Creating the book when you're finished with the draft requires spending money. In the previous chapter, I discussed the steps to take your manuscript from draft to final. Developmental editing, line/copy editing, and proofreading all cost money and must be factored in as one-time expenses. As mentioned earlier, developmental editors can cost anywhere from a few hundred to a few thousand dollars, depending on their experience, and line/copy editors might cost around one cent per word; proofreaders are usually about half that. If you have a short 50,000-word cozy mystery or romance novel, your book will cost much less to edit than a 90,000-word crime fiction novel or a 120,000-word epic fantasy.

THE COST OF CONVERTING YOUR FINAL MANUSCRIPT TO A SELLABLE BOOK

Your final manuscript, whether in Microsoft Word, Google Docs, or Scrivener, is not ready to be sold on book retailers or purchased by readers. You will have to do the work—or hire people—to transform that document into ebook, print, and audio formats.

First, you'll need to decide what formats you want to sell in: ebook, paperback, hardback, and audio. While many authors would love to see their names on a beautiful hardbound edition nestled among their favorite writers on a prominent display as they walk into a large chain bookstore, I hate to tell you that isn't a realistic goal as a self-published indie author. If you decide to sell print books, set your expectations to sell almost all of them through online retailers.

CREATING AN EBOOK

Unless you're a children's author or you write puzzle books, cookbooks, or other books where it's desirable to interact with the printed page, you'll publish in ebook format. Currently, all major retailers accept the EPUB format as their preferred ebook format. There are a wide variety of both paid and free software tools that can take a Microsoft Word document and convert it to EPUB. Ebooks are the easiest format for an author to create, and since EPUB creation is easy to learn and free (or low-cost), ebooks should be the priority format for you.

There are two things you must do to create a sellable ebook format: create the *ebook cover* and create the *ebook interior*.

For your ebook cover, you must meet your readers' expectations of a cover that looks indistinguishable from a traditionally published book, and it must look like a book in the genre that you are writing.

Sometimes, beginning authors can focus too much on their cover, particularly those who write science fiction or fantasy. I know some authors who commissioned original art for their first book covers for thousands of dollars. They were very happy with the result, but when the book was released, several of them realized they missed the mark with the instructions they gave the artist.

In most writing tools (Microsoft Word, Google Docs, and others), you can apply *paragraph styles* to different paragraphs in your book, add page and section breaks, and more. Familiarize yourself with these formatting options. Create page breaks before chapter headers, and pick an appropriate heading paragraph style for your chapter headers. Choose appropriate paragraph styles for unusual sections of your manuscript, such as text-message conversations, letters, signs, and so forth. Don't force formatting with spaces or tabs. When you import your manuscript into these conversion tools, those paragraph styles will usually convert your text appropriately, but forced tabs and spaces will result in a formatting nightmare. This is especially true for free tools.

If you'd like to use free tools to turn your manuscript into an ebook, I recommend Calibre and Kindle Create. If you have any background in HTML programming, there are other tools like Jutoh that provide much more control. If you don't mind spending some money, a tool called Atticus is available that provides a much richer experience with lots of options for fonts, headings, and so forth. I prefer a Mac-only software program called Vellum, but I didn't purchase that until I wrote my fourth book.

CREATING OTHER FORMATS

In a Chapter 4, I said that most successful self-published books look indistinguishable from traditionally published books, especially when your book is placed next to many others in an online bookstore. Part of that level of professionalism is having the book available in different formats. Some experts believe that when a reader sees a page where the book is only available as an ebook (assuming the retailers sells different formats), it subconsciously signals a book of lesser quality. As far as I can tell, there haven't been any studies on this, but Harvard Business School professor Gerald Zaltman believes that 95% of purchasing decisions are made by "the subconscious mind." If readers subconsciously notice that their favorite traditionally published authors have paperbacks, hardbacks, and audiobooks in addition to ebooks, if you only have an ebook available that might negatively impact their decision to buy.

In addition, audiobook sales are growing at a much faster pace than the rest of the book market. Revenue from audiobooks, according to studies compiled by Nicholas Rizzo of WordsRated, is expected to grow by almost 25% annually for the next four years. Most statistics available for the book market will imply that print books are still dominating the market as well, and print book sales have also grown in double figures since a low-water mark in 2012.

However, many of the reports focus solely on what publishers report—which skews the data toward traditionally published titles. These statistics also cover the entire book market; the genre you write in may be significantly different. Deciding which formats to publish will need to be done with incomplete data.

Additional costs factor in creating other formats, as well. Ebook covers cost much less than full paperback and hardback designs. Creating the interior file of a print book is different than the interior of an ebook, and may require additional investment, either in dedicated software like Vellum, Atticus, or even Adobe InDesign, or by hiring someone who can make the interior of your print book look professional.

Almost all indie authors produce their print books using "print-on-demand" services, which are then sold directly through either online book retailers or to brick-and-mortar stores from the print-on-demand service. That means, fortunately, there is no longer a need to pay for the upfront printing of thousands of print copies. Multiple vendors (and many options) are available to produce both paperback and hardback editions. The price you pay to print a book comes directly out of your royalties for the book; for example, if you sell your book for $20, you may get 45% of the sale price ($9), and your print-on-demand cost comes out of that $9. Depending on the length, size, paper choice, and color requirements of your book, you might keep between $3 and $6 for most typical print books.

For print, you might also consider large-print books (i.e., with a font size of at least 16 point). If you write in a genre that skews more toward older readers, such as cozy mystery or sweet romance, this could be a lucrative option, particularly if you decide to sell to libraries. I have an author friend who makes over $100,000 per year, and half her sales are large-print print books; I have other author friends who sell in genres that skew older who sell just a handful of large-print books a year. Again, every author's journey is different.

The cost of print production includes getting a "full" cover file that is a single "sheet" including the back cover, spine, and front cover. These must be submitted as PDF files with exact dimensions (and the companies are very inflexible regarding their expectations). You can submit to Amazon KDP, IngramSpark, Barnes & Noble Print, Draft2Digital, and others. Professional cover designers will often provide a full cover file and an ebook cover together for about twice the price of an ebook cover. There are authors who do covers themselves, but it requires special software, artistic talent, and attention to detail that most authors don't have. I worked for years in my early career as a graphic designer, but I still hire a cover designer for this. You'll need the final page count for your book before creating a print-ready cover (because of the width of the spine). Follow the specific instructions for your vendor, and be aware that although you can submit to multiple vendors, different vendors use different materials (and therefore may require final PDFs of different sizes). Adding a large-print cover to your regular print cover will add more cost, but it will be a fraction of the price of a new cover.

Print books will require a design for the interior of your book as well. Some authors have had successful sales formatting the interior of their books with Microsoft Word, but in my experience, it's difficult for word processing programs to make the interior of print books look professional. There are dedicated programs like Vellum and Atticus for this, as well as free tools from Draft2Digital and Reedsy. You can also use professional page layout programs such as Adobe InDesign for this work, which provide the most control and fewest limitations—but also require the most knowledge and the most time. Vellum and Atticus are purpose-built for authors to do the interior layout themselves; I believe that Vellum delivers results professional enough to use for my own self-published books. If buying your own software doesn't appeal to you, hiring someone to create the interior of your text-only book usually costs under $150, but if you have needs like graphics, color, special formatting, or other "outside-the-box" requests, you may pay quite a bit.

The cost of print production doesn't even come close to that for audiobooks. The cost of hiring a narrator can be steep, as many professionals charge $300 or more "per finished hour" of the audiobook. (If your book is 10 hours long, the narration will cost $3,000, for example.) This seems high if you believe the narrator just hits record, starts to read, then 10 hours later they're done—but that's not the case. Narrators have often invested thousands of dollars into equipment and sound booths, will often need to spend hours editing and re-recording sections, and must prepare the audio files so that the audiobook retailers will accept them.

If you believe that you can read the book yourself, remember that the quality of your book needs to be indistinguishable from a traditionally published audiobook.

That means no audible background noise, a clear and pleasant voice to listen to, and appropriate variance of your tone (it helps if you have a theater background). It means investing in a quality microphone (try out microphones if you do this; your voice may sound great on a $100 mike but awful on a $2,000 mike, or vice versa), audio equipment, a computer and software to record everything, and a place where you can record in silence without echo (which might require soundproofing). If you have a theater background and a walk-in closet large enough, you might be able to do it yourself. Remember, too, that your ten-hour audiobook will likely take 40 or 50 hours to record, and probably more than that the first time you do it. You'll also need to factor in "proof-listening" and re-recording time.

When you are a new indie author, maximizing your investments and starting small can save you both time and money. Based on all the factors above, I decided to start with ebooks and paperbacks. Some of my author friends write mysteries like I do, and they sell thousands of print books every month. One author makes over $1,000 a month just from large-print sales. However, my author journey is different; 98% of my sales are ebooks, not print. I am just starting with audiobook production, also, and it's going much slower than I thought it would.

If you're just starting out, I would suggest starting with ebooks and paperbacks; I'm unconvinced that hardbacks and audio are good investments for indie authors who aren't making $1,000 a month yet.

MY EXPERIENCE: THE COST OF CREATING MY FIRST NOVEL

When you are first starting out, it might be difficult to get—or to justify spending—thousands of dollars on all these costs. I was able to minimize my "startup" costs in some areas; many other authors who have been successful did much of their early work themselves. Here were my expenses:

- **Manuscript:** I already owned a laptop and a copy of Microsoft Word, so I didn't need to invest in a computer or writing software.
- **Developmental and line editor**: I found a not-very-experienced editor who gave me three edits—two for story structure and one for line editing—for $750 (and remember, that was in 2018 dollars). While I have since found it much more effective to have separate developmental and line editors, at the time I didn't think I could justify the expense for my first book.
- **Proofreading**: I skimped on this, as I have several friends who are English teachers, and they proofread my book. If I knew then what I know now, I would have asked them to follow *The Chicago Manual of Style*, which is what most traditionally published novels in the United States follow. Using my friends

meant proofreading was free for me, but because I didn't pay a professional, quite a few errors were caught by readers after publication. (Fortunately, when you self-publish books, you can edit them whenever you want.)

- **Interior design of ebook and print book:** I used to work as a production designer early in my career, and I had the skills necessary to do the interior design myself. For the ebook, I used the free Amazon's Kindle Create and Calibre—and it didn't take any special skills. For the print book, however, I do believe it required the knowledge I had from typesetting and graphic design. I used Adobe InDesign, which I had been using for years, and took about five days to create the print book interior. If you need to pay for this, you can get the print interior designed for $150 or less, which might also include the ebook interior.
- **Cover design:** I was also lucky in this area. I have a good friend who has been an art director for decades. He came up with a great idea for the cover (the title of the book in yellow police caution tape), and I've used him for every cover design since. Because he and I are friends, I paid him for my first few covers

in bourbon; now I pay him the going rate for cover designers. (If I had not used him, I would have tried to find a cover from the many websites that offer pre-made covers; I would have budgeted $300.)

PART TWO
EFFECTIVE MARKETING

CHAPTER 8
YOUR BOOK IS AN ADVERTISEMENT, NOT A PRODUCT

ONCE YOU'VE WRITTEN a book that you believe will meet reader expectations—and you may have one right now that's either published or soon-to-be-published—that's the first thing that you want people to read: The introduction to your work. For many authors, this is their Entry Point Novel. (I'll refer to this "first book you want people to read" as a "Entry Point Novel.")

If you're like many authors, you think of your Entry Point Novel as a **product**—a product you may love, and a product you believe has great value.

And why wouldn't you think of your book like this? You've seen other authors with Entry Point Novels that fly up the bestseller charts. And you worked *hard* to write this book, right? A lot of writers put years of effort into their first novels. Like me, you might think you'll be the next Angie Thomas or Carson McCullers: a novelist whose first book changes the literary scene and sets you up for a satisfying writing career.

But that won't happen to you.

Statistically speaking, while it's rare for a traditionally published Entry Point Novel to hit those heights, it's almost impossible for a self-published Entry Point Novel to sell that well—and it's only getting harder.

Not only will your Entry Point Novel not sell a million copies, it isn't even a product.

Your Entry Point Novel is, instead, the best advertisement for your writing.

The best advertisement for all your *other* books.

"Hang on," you may be saying, "I wrote a book. I want to sell the book. I didn't write an *ad* for my other books. What are you talking about?"

If you treat your Entry Point Novel like a product and not an advertisement, you may have a much harder time selling your books—any books—in your catalog. Self-published books are different than traditionally published books.

Traditional publishers have marketing teams to sell their products. They have relationships with distributors who can place those Entry Point Novels in big bookseller chains in a display at the front of the store. They have the contacts to place those Entry Point Novels in airport bookshops. They don't just throw Entry Point Novels up on the ebook retailer websites and hope for the best: they actively promote the books they believe in, and they're (sometimes) masters at pushing their products.

But self-published books are different. Without the marketing machine of a big publisher, self-published authors are at a disadvantage when it comes to getting their books in front of their potential audience. You don't have a contact who can put a display of your novel at the front of every store of a nationwide chain.

But, just like traditional publishers, you can't just throw your Entry Point Novel up on ebook retailer websites and wait for the cash to roll in. Hundreds of new books are appearing on these book retailer sites every day. Without a strategy to get your books—not just your Entry Point Novel, but *all* your books—in front of readers, you'll have trouble selling much of anything.

Thinking back to the last chapter, put yourself in the shoes of your readers. Don't limit your thinking to the way *you* choose to buy books, either. Think of your friends and family members who read: how do they find the books they buy?

There are many kinds of readers. In the romance reader community, it's not uncommon to find "whale readers"—people who burn through one or more books every day. But they're the exception—and whale readers are uncommon outside the romance genre. The average person only reads one book a year, and even those who enjoy reading for pleasure only choose ten or twelve books every year.

What this means is that most readers choose their books carefully. They're not just making a monetary decision: they're making a commitment to spend five to ten hours with the novel they decide to purchase. Readers often agonize over the decision of **what to read next**.

Indie authors' books may cost less than a grande Frappuccino, but it's not the same. A book will demand the undivided attention of the reader, and a fiction reader is often looking for an emotional connection to the book: something that will make them feel better than they did before they started the book. (I'm not talking about requiring happy endings or typical "feel-good" plots—even tragic tear-jerker books make readers feel better about themselves for having read the book.) A five-dollar coffee drink will warm you up, cool you down, or give you a burst of energy —and that's worth five dollars to many consumers. A five-dollar ebook might entertain you for six hours, but it might also frustrate you, bore you, or waste six hours of your life —and as a seller, it's a higher hurdle to clear. It's also why many readers will choose to spend twenty-five dollars on a traditionally published book rather than five dollars on an indie author's ebook: because the publisher has spent time and effort making sure the book delivers on its promise to readers. Even with the hiring of professional editors, a thorough beta-reading process, and an army of proofreaders, self-published authors sometimes can't deliver on that promise. (See my horror stories from Chapter Seven.)

This is a daunting challenge for self-published authors—but the good news is that if readers like your Entry Point Novel, it makes their decision of **what to read next** easier. (It's less easy for readers if you write in different genres under the same name; it's much easier for readers if you write in the same series.) Seasoned indie authors will often talk about their readthrough rate from their Entry Point Novel to their second book. A much higher percentage of readers who buy that second book will buy the third book. If the author has maintained a consistent voice and likeable characters, a very high percentage of third-book readers will go on to purchase the rest of your books—especially if your books are in the same series.

That's why you need to treat your Entry Point Novel like the greatest advertisement for writing that you'll have.

Advertising is a tried-and-true way to sell products. Advertising has two essential elements: **reach** and **persuasiveness**.

- *Reach*: the more people who see the advertisement, the more people will buy the product
- *Persuasiveness*: the more convincing the ad is, the more people will buy the product

While there are many differences between a self-published author business and other consumer products, *reach* and *persuasiveness* are still essential.

- *Reach*: your Entry Point Novel needs to reach as many potential readers as possible

- *Persuasiveness*: your Entry Point Novel needs to effectively persuade those readers to buy your next book

You're not selling snack foods or toothpaste or a common consumer item that everyone buys. Readers are a small fraction of the public, and the readers who would consider the genre you write in is even smaller than that.

Unlike snack food or toothpaste companies, authors won't be effective creating an ad and buying ad placement on television or streaming services or a billboard. That might get your advertisement for your book seen by a large number of people, but it won't be the *right* people —it won't be the people most likely to buy your books.

Facebook, Amazon, and BookBub will sell authors ad placement specifically to targeted readers. There are some great books by experts like M.D. Cooper and David Gaughran on how to make those ads effective.

While Facebook, Amazon, and BookBub ads can be part of an effective self-publishing marketing strategy, it often requires a lot more money than beginning authors can spend. Testing ads and tweaking them until they become effective cost me thousands of dollars—and I can't advocate that strategy for self-published authors who are only making a handful of sales.

PRODUCT SAMPLING AS ADVERTISING

In grocery stores or in membership big-box stores, companies will often send representatives to set up a table, prepare food in-store, and give small amounts of that food to shoppers who pass by. This is a marketing strategy known as **product sampling.**

The potential customers can try the food without committing to a purchase. Marketer Ali Reyes describes product sampling's purpose as a strategy "to build customers' trust in your newly launched product so they can purchase it later without any doubt."

Reyes also states that free samples can dramatically increase sales—up to 2000%.

As with any marketing strategy, there are risks to free samples. Most importantly, as marketing expert Curt Cleveland says, that free sample must be "of high quality so it can bring back the customers." If the food sample isn't tasty, consumers won't buy the whole bag.

The advertising strategy of giving out free food samples in grocery stores (or any sort of physical product sample) is also expensive. Companies must pay for the food; they must hire someone to prepare the food and staff the table; in many cases, they may have to pay that store for the time and floor space. Free sampling can be an expensive advertising strategy. Some companies offer their product samples not for free, but at a significantly reduced price that allows them to recoup some of their expenses.

Another risk of product sampling is "freebie-seekers"—consumers who have absolutely no intention of spending any money but who go to stuff their faces with free food. These people are often sneaky, trying to get multiple samples. They can be hostile when confronted, and often act entitled. (Offering the product samples for a reduced price usually puts an end to this behavior.)

Despite the risks, product sampling is a very effective marketing strategy. Not only can it immediately establish trust with the buyer, but the advertising is also *in* the purchase location, so there's little chance of the consumer forgetting about the sample before the purchase decision.

You may not think of product sampling as advertising, but that's exactly what it is. The company is meeting their potential customers very close to the point of sale and providing, for no cost, a taste of their product. Some companies may charge a small fee for a taste of their product (many wineries, for instance, now offer a few sips of their wine for a low price rather than free).

Whether offered for free or at low cost, product sampling as an advertising strategy means that customers know exactly what they're getting, and the whole point of the sample is to get customers to purchase the whole bag of pizza snacks, the whole bottle of kale smoothie, or the whole case of cabernet sauvignon.

For self-published authors, I encourage you to consider using product sampling as an advertising strategy—and think of that Entry Point Novel as a delicious treat for the shoppers passing your table in the aisles.

PRODUCT SAMPLING FOR AUTHORS: FEWER DOWNSIDES

In the virtual world, product sampling works much the same way. Instead of a grocery store, consumers visit a website and sign up to receive a sample of a product. The company, at their cost, sends a sample of that product to the consumer in the hopes that they'll purchase more.

For self-published authors, using product sampling as advertising has all the advantages with far fewer disadvantages.

Advantages:

- Consumers can try your writing without committing to a purchase.
- Trust is built with potential buyers if the sample is of high quality.
- Advertising is often very close to purchase location, making the purchase of the next book easy.

Disadvantages of product sampling that do not affect authors:

- Ebooks cost nothing to give away (as opposed to physical products).
- Authors do not have to hire staff to give ebooks away.

Though some disadvantages still apply:

- A low-quality sample can break consumer trust and will not increase sales.
- Freebie-seekers will still attempt to get as much stuff for free as they can.

Most people have experienced going by a food sample table at a grocery or big-box store, having a sample, and thinking it was so delicious they decide to get a full package or bag. In many cases, the consumer wasn't even considering that item before they tried the sample.

Even if you don't partake in free samples for whatever reason, you've seen others do it. The free sample immediately persuades that person to buy the product.

That's why getting your Entry Point Novel into the hands of a member of your target audience is so important: because that book is the most persuasive advertisement there is to get sales to the rest of your catalog.

Whether you're offering your Entry Point Novel for free or at a reduced price, readers will only be convinced to take your book for a test drive. Once they choose your book, they've only chosen it to see if it's something that suits them. They might give up in the first ten percent of the book. They might even give up on the first page. They might be on a buying or downloading spree and never even open your book.

So that book must be a great advertisement for the rest of your series or the rest of your catalog—it must be of a high enough quality to establish trust with the reader that your books are worth their time, money, and emotional investment.

THE AD IS IMPORTANT, BUT THE QUALITY OF THE BOOK IS CRUCIAL

If the books that you've written aren't good quality, it won't matter too much how good your advertisement/Entry Point Novel is. In fact, advertising legend Bill Bernbach famously said, "A great ad campaign will make a bad product fail faster."

Bernbach's quote was never more accurate than with the 1993 Crystal Pepsi debacle. With a dynamic and creative minute-long television spot placed during the Super Bowl, Crystal Pepsi showcased its clear (not brown) cola, emotionally connecting with viewers. Using Van Halen's hit song "Right Now," the ad touted many possibilities, alluded to some of the problems, and thematically connected forward-thinking values to the product: "artificial doesn't feel right," "only wildlife needs preservatives," "we're all thirsty for something different," and many other short sayings—all connected with "right now." (Almost no one remembers this ad, but search online for "Crystal Pepsi ad"—you'll see the launch ad in all its 1990s glory.)

But less than a year after that triumphant launch, Crystal Pepsi—which experts expected to be a billion-dollar seller—was discontinued. Twenty years later, Thrillist dubbed Crystal Pepsi a "colossal flop," and *Time Magazine* called it one of the biggest product launch failures in history. What happened?

While the media has written many articles analyzing what went wrong, in the end, I believe the failure comes down to **meeting customer expectations**. The product didn't taste enough like cola, and there was (and still is) an expectation that cola is brown, not clear. The product also "spoiled" quickly in heat and direct sunlight—which *definitely* didn't meet customer expectations of taking a cold drink to a kids' soccer game or the beach on a hot day.

In contrast, many advertising experts agree that one of the greatest ads ever was the "1984" ad for the first Apple Macintosh computer. Helmed by famous movie director Ridley Scott, the ad was striking; many media pundits went so far as to call it revolutionary. (Search online for "1984 Apple commercial" if you haven't seen it.)

But the ad wouldn't be perceived as successful without a good quality product behind it. Fortunately, the Macintosh computer *delivered* on the advertisement's promise to consumers. Without a good product, a great ad becomes ineffective and forgotten.

It should be clear how important it is for all your "follow-up products"—all the other books in the series—to be just as high-quality as the product sample in your advertising. If the free mini tacos were better than those in the bags of mini tacos for sale, complaints would rise—and sales would fall. That's not good for buyers *or* companies. So when you write another book in your catalog or series, keep in mind how important it is to meet those reader expectations of the genre.

There are multiple reasons why many experts say that writing another great book is the most important "marketing activity" you can do. Because when a reader gets to the end of one of your books—whether it's the book you treat like an ad or another book in your catalog—you want them to immediately buy and read the next book in the series. The more books in your series and the more books in your catalog, the more money each "free sample" has the potential to earn.

And, most importantly, when you start to think of your Entry Point Novel as a product sample and not like an invaluable, precious artwork, a world of marketing possibilities open up.

CHAPTER 9
TURNING YOUR BOOK INTO AN ADVERTISEMENT

YOU MAY SEE the value of turning your book into an advertisement for the rest of your series. But you might be skeptical of what I mean by "think of your book as an advertisement."

Of course, I'm not talking about turning the book into an actual YouTube ad or an Amazon sponsored ad.

So how *do* you turn your book into an advertisement?

STEP ONE: THE HOOK

An issue common to many first-in-series books: taking far too long to set up the inciting incident—the event that occurs to set the story in motion, placing the main character squarely in the middle of the action.

There are a few reasons why authors might choose to take a long time before the inciting incident. One is that for many people, their first-in-series is the first novel they've ever written (even if it's not, it's often an early attempt) and early work often meanders in the first few chapters. New authors often spend a long time introducing the setting, the main character, or the forces at play. For fantasy and sci-fi authors, worldbuilding can be overexplained early in the narrative. I've seen some new authors go on for sixty or seventy pages with characters who *die* at the end of those chapters, all as backstory to set up the main character and the inciting incident. More than a few times, I've read a first novel that spends several chapters without any plot at all.

Advertisements don't do this. Advertisers know—especially today, in the world of "Skip Ad" buttons, that they have to grab the viewer at the get-go. Even something as seemingly innocent as a famous celebrity saying, "Hello, my name is Famous Celebrity Name" will get people clicking on the skip button.

While your book doesn't follow today's advertising rule of "grab 'em in the first two seconds," you as an author have to engage your reader quickly. It doesn't mean that you must have something incredibly shocking, embarrassing, or violent in the first paragraph. But it does mean that you need to give the reader a reason to care about your characters and introduce an interesting conflict early—yes, preferably in the first few pages. There are simply too many other books (and Netflix shows) out there for readers to be patient with authors who take their time getting to interesting conflict between characters they care about.

When I first made my Entry Point Novel—the first

Fenway Stevenson novel—free, I had a huge opportunity for a big promotion: I could get the free book in front of thousands of readers, and the promo was scheduled in three weeks' time. Excited about this fantastic opportunity, I told Max Christian Hansen, my editor.

But was Max excited? Nope.

He said the book wasn't good enough to get in front of thousands of readers. In fact, he *insisted* that I rewrite the first seven chapters of my Entry Point Novel.

I was shocked—and I asked him to convince me why I needed to make such extensive changes.

Max told me that I had done what I admonished against a few paragraphs ago: I spent far too long meandering. Fenway Stevenson's conflict with her father wasn't very strong in the first chapter. Her personal goals weren't clear in the first fifty or sixty pages. Even the scenes in chapters four and five that should have been rife with conflict were unfocused. As I was rewriting those chapters, I cringed as I read what I'd originally published. It became evident that I wasn't clear with Fenway's goals because when I wrote those early chapters, I didn't know what she wanted. After chapter eight or so, her goals started to solidify, but those first seven chapters were poorly written. Even so, I was treating the book like a product, like a work of art, and not like an ad for the rest of my series. I had made excuses for my meandering narrative rather than treating my Entry Point Novel like an advertisement for the rest of my series.

After editing, the pace was snappier, Fenway Stevenson's goals were clear, and the conflict with her father was at the forefront. It helped the rest of the book seem more cohesive, too, because I had now set the audience's expectations properly.

This is what a good advertisement does: it intrigues, it entertains, and it establishes the audience's expectations about what they'll experience when they buy the product. If you as the author are promising an unfocused, sprawling narrative absent a propulsive conflict, then that's what audiences are going to expect the rest of your books to be. And if that's the case, it will negatively affect your sales.

STEP TWO: THE LOOK

This piece of advice has been given by self-publishing experts for years, but it bears repeating: your self-published book must look indistinguishable from a traditionally published book in the genre. A reader should look at your cover, blurb, and opening pages and be unable to tell that it's self-published.

Again, this has everything to do with what you're promising your audience. Are you promising them a quality read or not? Is your manuscript full of grammatical, spelling, and punctuation errors? Or is the grammar and punctuation indistinguishable from the latest book from Penguin Random House?

One of the great advantages of being self-published is that there are no gatekeepers to tell you that they don't think they can make money on your vampire romance. But the flip side of this is that there's no one to tell you when your book doesn't look professional either. And authors are notoriously bad at self-editing, cover design, interior design, and sales descriptions. (There are a few exceptions—but even then, if you're good at one or two of those things, you're probably not good at all of them, especially early in your author career.)

That's why it's important to hire editors, designers, proofreaders, and copywriters to do that work for you. Experts will tell you that you must put your best foot forward—but what you're really doing is putting a professional looking advertisement together. Look at the ads featured on YouTube or on TV: they're cohesive and professional—and they cost money to create. (There are some exceptions to this—take those Snapple ad campaigns of the late 1990s, for example. Those ads looked DIY and lo-fi, and although a big ad agency had written them, they cost much less to create than typical ads. Likewise, there are authors whose grammar is terrible, whose covers look amateurish, and whose blurbs aren't compelling who **still** do well in their sales. But, again, those people are the exceptions, and you'll be making success harder for yourself if you scrimp on these areas.)

If you treat your first book like an advertisement, you'll be putting yourself in the best position to succeed. If you don't, you'll be putting obstacles in front of your sales.

CHAPTER 10
SPENDING MONEY TO MAKE MONEY

AN ANCIENT ROMAN playwright named Titus Maccius Plautus is credited with saying, "You have to spend money to make money." It's an annoying cliché—made more annoying because it's true.

You cannot simply write your books and toss the Microsoft Word files up on the bookseller sites and watch the money roll in.

In the last chapter, we discussed how treating your Entry Point Novel as an advertisement can put you in the best position to succeed. But implementing this strategy, unfortunately, comes with a price tag.

Any company that creates a product must figure out how to package that product: whether it's a generic paper box or a custom-designed jewel-encrusted crystal case, packaging is crucial to meeting the customer's expectation and convincing them to buy.

Likewise, the company must figure out how to get their product in front of the people who will purchase.

This concept has two parts: one is deciding *where* to sell the products. A cookie company has a different set of customer expectations selling in stores like Whole Foods, Waitrose, or Harris Farm Markets compared to Aldi, Asda, or WinCo. As an author, selling on certain e-retailers may not cost you money, but could affect how much you make for each book purchased.

The second part of getting the product in front of an audience is advertising, and if advertisements are in that mix, the company needs to spend money. They need the advertisement developed, and they need to spend money with websites, social media sites, or traditional media to get their product and message across to their audience.

Many book marketing experts will discuss the role of Amazon, Facebook, or BookBub ads, but unless you're already making more than $1,000 a month, these ads are impractical. Instead, upcoming chapters will discuss ways to get the word out about your books with significantly lower costs.

CHAPTER 11
WHERE WILL YOU SELL YOUR BOOKS?

PART of a successful marketing strategy for self-published fiction is determining where to sell your books.

For companies that sell mobile phones, cookware, or exercise equipment, this means getting their products into brick-and-mortar stores or building their own stores. For indie authors, it's similar—except almost everything is online. The biggest retailers are websites, and you can set up your own author store on the web too.

Some websites are much better for certain genres of books, some websites have the ability to sell more than just ebooks (e.g., audio and print), and some websites have different models for pricing.

The "big five" of ebook retailers are:

- Amazon (with stores set up for different countries and regions)
- Apple Books

- Barnes & Noble (as of this writing, its customers must reside in the USA)
- Kobo
- Google Play

KU OR WIDE?

One of the first decisions you'll need to make when you publish your first book is "KU or wide?" And, because it's a decision that needs to be made so early in the publishing process, most authors make this decision before understanding—or even knowing—the long-term ramifications it can have to their marketing strategy.

KU stands for "Kindle Unlimited," a subscription service where, for $10 a month, Amazon users can read any ebook that is enrolled in the KU program for no additional cost; for indie authors, this requires ebook exclusivity to Amazon. "Wide" means that you distribute your ebook to multiple retailers.

HOW DOES KU WORK?

In Amazon's Kindle Direct Publishing (KDP) dashboard, the author will enroll the book in "KDP Select" to get their book eligible for KU. KDP Select is a 90-day program where you commit to your ebook remaining exclusive to Amazon for that 90-day period. In return, you get access to KU. There are several advantages to being in KU.

First, the money. When a KU subscriber reads your book, you get about 40-45% of one U.S. cent for every page that a KU user reads (the payout changes every month). This is commonly referred to as "page reads." For a 90,000-word book, this equates to a little over $2, give or take.

You also get access to these KU subscribers; they are often readers who might not otherwise read your books—and this might include some of the "freebie seekers" out there. Many KU authors make a lot of money through page reads.

There are a couple of other perks, too. Amazon gives you 70% of your unit sales in most of the world, there are a few countries (as of this writing, those countries include Brazil, Japan, Mexico, and India) that net you 35% royalties—unless your ebooks are in KDP Select; then you get 70%.

Finally, Amazon allows every book enrolled in KDP Select to be offered for promotional pricing—often free for a few days—out of every 90-day KDP Select cycle.

The disadvantages: you must make your ebook exclusive to Amazon, and you must abide by Amazon's strict and fairly complex rules (both written and unwritten). This means that you cannot sell the ebook on any other retailer—including your own website. You cannot distribute your book through BookFunnel or StoryOrigin. You cannot distribute any title with any significant section of the KDP Select-enrolled book to other retailers or your own website. (So, for example, you cannot publish Book 1 wide if you enroll a collection of Books 1-3 in KDP Select.) And I have heard anecdotes about Amazon finding an author's books on a pirate website and shutting down the author's account.

You can exit KDP Select after each 90-day enrollment period; some authors have emailed Amazon, asked to be removed from KDP Select, and been released before their enrollment period ended; other authors, however, have *not* been released from their agreements.

Amazon exclusivity is limited to ebooks. Your print books and audiobooks can go wide even if your ebook is enrolled in KDP Select.

HOW DOES AN AUTHOR GO WIDE?

All the major retail sites have dashboards that allow you to upload your book, including the title, description, cover art, EPUB file, pricing (often for multiple countries), book categories, and more. Simply uploading and publishing your book to multiple sites is "going wide." As long as you *don't* enroll your book in KDP Select when you upload your book to Amazon (or if you leave the KDP Select program), you can go wide.

The advantage of going wide is getting access to the millions of readers on the non-Amazon platforms, and in the dozens of countries to which Amazon does not distribute ebooks. You also won't have all your eggs in the Amazon basket; I have heard horror stories of authors who are exclusive to Amazon who have had their accounts terminated. The authors often say they don't know what they did wrong, and their author income is now gone.

The disadvantage of going wide is primarily that you don't have access to the KU program (or the readers who exclusively read KU books). From an administrative standpoint, it's also much more work to upload your book to multiple storefronts—you must make sure your prices match across all the countries and regions as well.

Kobo and Google Play are both very strong in sales outside the USA. Kobo is based in Canada, and offers a subscription service, similar to KU, to its readers in Canada, the U.K., and several other countries. You must enroll your books in "Kobo Plus" to take advantage of this, and unlike KU, Kobo Plus does **not** require exclusivity. Google Play allows your books to be sold in most countries around the world, offering pricing and distribution options to countries that Amazon, Apple Books, and even Kobo don't.

There are other companies, often called **aggregators**, that will take care of all the uploading and pricing on many different stores (not just the big names). These aggregators, such as Draft2Digital, PublishDrive, and StreetLib, are sometimes the only way you can get into libraries and onto stores in non-English-speaking countries (if you're based in the USA, the aggregators are the only way I know to get access to Tolino and Vivlio, for example). Some aggregators will take a percentage of your sales; some charge a flat monthly fee. Note that there are some e-retailers who will provide specific promotional opportunities to authors who go direct that the retailer doesn't make available to aggregators (as of this writing, Kobo and Barnes & Noble are two examples of retailers who have exclusive promotional opportunities for many of their direct authors).

You can also sell your ebooks (and print and audiobooks, too) directly from your website. With this model, you keep a much higher percentage of each sale (usually over 90%, as opposed to the 35-70% from the retailers; you only pay for the payment processing). Taking on this strategy depends on your ability to create websites and your desire to manage third-party storefronts and financial applications. For most authors starting out, I don't recommend this—unless you have a strong idea how to get readers to your website. If you don't have experience with e-commerce, it's a lot of work for (usually) not a lot of revenue, although I do recommend building your online store after you've built a readership. (Many books, classes, and resources are available on "selling direct," but most authors won't see a big bump before they're making $1,000 a month, so I won't discuss this topic further.)

RECOMMENDATIONS: KU VS. WIDE

Personally, I publish wide. I go direct to Amazon, Kobo, Barnes & Noble, and Google Play, and I use an aggregator for Apple Books (one of the few stores that allows, as of this writing, promotional opportunities to aggregators), libraries, and other stores. However, many authors make good money being in the KDP Select program and being exclusive to Amazon. There's also a matter of what you can tolerate in terms of administration and management: many people dislike the extra work that going wide requires. In short, KU versus wide is a personal decision, and many factors contribute to whether you'll be successful in each distribution strategy.

Some people believe that KU is better for some genres and wide is better for others. Romance, for example, is commonly cited in indie author groups as being more KU-friendly. I don't believe your genre is as important as your attitude toward the limitations and opportunities that KDP Select's exclusivity places on your marketing strategy.

Whatever you decide, I strongly recommend that you don't bounce between the two. If your books are in KU, your readers will come to expect your books to be in KU. If your books are available on other sites, your readers will expect your books to be available on the other sites. If you've spent six months wide and sell very little on non-Amazon stores, and you don't want to spend the extra time to publish and promote to other stores, by all means, go to KU. (Make sure the aggregators have gotten your books out of all the different stores!) But don't bounce back and forth every 90 days—you'll anger all your readers, and that's not a good way to build your author business to $1,000 a month. You'll also annoy the employees of the wide storefronts, who sometimes select books for their promotions. If they're not sure if your books are going to be on their storefront, they won't choose you.

Many indie authors—myself included—started out in KU before going wide. Publishing that first novel can seem like a steep learning curve, and having one e-retailer to deal with (Amazon) compared to five (or more) seems much less overwhelming. After the first 90-day exclusivity period, I was disappointed with my page reads, and I had more time and energy to devote to the other e-retailers, so I discontinued my enrollment in KDP Select and went wide.

CHAPTER 12
PROMOTING YOUR BOOK

THERE ARE two components of promotional advertising for authors to be able to successfully promote their books. The first is the "advertisement" itself, and the second is the vehicle you use to get the advertisement in front of your audience.

Successful companies rarely, if ever, create ads that aren't professionally developed—and for good reason. Ads that don't look professional are generally less successful than professionally developed ads. And companies rarely, if ever, throw a product into the world's marketplace without some way of letting people know the product exists.

It's the same with your author business. As discussed in the last chapter, your best advertisement—your book—must be professionally developed, and you must get that ad in front of your target audience.

If you want to make $1,000 a month from your self-published books, you must do the math to determine what you can afford to invest and where you can most effectively invest it.

Many beginning writers are in the same boat: they can afford little, if any, money to go toward editing, cover design, and marketing, but as discussed in Chapters 7 and 10, spending a certain amount of money is usually required to get your book where it needs to be—both in terms of quality *and* in front of potential readers.

THE IMPORTANCE OF COVERS

It's of paramount importance that **your cover match your readers' expectations for books in the genre that you're writing in**. You may think of book covers as part of the product, but they are the first thing readers see that helps sell the book—covers make a first impression on the reader, and usually you don't get another chance to impress the reader.

You may have heard the cliché "don't judge a book by its cover," but that's a cliché precisely because every single reader *does* judge books by their covers. That cliché's advice is for readers, not authors—and it's almost never taken!

As illustrated by my experience with the *Murders of Substance* series, creating covers that look different than the other covers in your genre can wreck your sales.

Especially with your Entry Point Novel, the cover is

the most important promotional piece you'll have. It's what readers who are shopping for a book see first—so if they pass you over because your action-adventure novel looks like a self-help book, you've already lost.

A good, professional, effective book cover can cost anywhere from $100 to $400. If you are looking for custom illustration or photography, your costs can rise significantly. Self-publishing experts can provide advice on how to edit and design covers on a budget.

Besides the design (and title) of the cover itself, you'll need to provide your author name on the cover. Many indie authors think that since no one knows who they are, they should put their name much smaller than the title of the book.

But take a look at your favorite book retailer's website and look at the bestseller lists there. All of them have the author name large enough to read in the thumbnail graphic of the book cover. Whatever you do with your book cover, make sure your title and author name are easy to read at thumbnail size. And don't be afraid of making your name large; while you may not be as well-known as the authors whose names are larger than their book titles, your job is to make your book cover look indistinguishable from a traditionally published book—not to give into your modesty or imposter syndrome. Besides, if you *do* get more popular, it will be easy for your readership to find your backlist titles.

GETTING YOUR BOOK IN FRONT OF READERS

And, while you think of your first book as an advertisement, you'll also have to promote your book to your audience. (Think of your Entry Point Novel as a company paying to have an ad created, then the book promotion like paying YouTube, Hulu, a TV network, or a website to run that ad.)

So now that you have your Entry Point Novel, how do you use that to get more book sales?

MAKE IT EASY FOR READERS TO GET YOUR NEXT BOOK

After the conclusion of your Entry Point Novel, immediately follow it with a preview containing the first two or three chapters of the next book in your series (or if you're a standalone writer, the next book you want your audience to read). Immediately following the last paragraph of your preview, create a link that takes people directly to purchase that second book.

NEWSLETTER LISTS

More than anything else, a list of readers (and their email addresses) is the most important thing you can have if you want to make $1,000 a month with your self-published fiction.

If you have a list of interested readers, you have a

ready-made audience for every announcement for your new releases, and if you have their email addresses, you have an easy way to contact them that's much cheaper than any other marketing tactic.

The biggest reason to have a newsletter list, though, is that **you own the list**. If you contact your readership primarily through a social media platform, you don't own that. If that platform kicks you off, if there's a big glitch, or if it changes its rules, you won't have any way to contact the readers you've connected with.

For authors who are just starting out, it's likely that you don't have a very long list—you might just have a few supportive friends and relatives.

The first thing I did to grow my book sales was use my Entry Point Novel to build my newsletter list. I started with two websites: an email marketing site where I could store my newsletter list, and BookFunnel, a website where I could attract readers to build that list.

CREATING AN EFFECTIVE NEWSLETTER

I find that my newsletter subscribers are by far my most reliable source of income—and the marketing vehicle of newsletters is also much cheaper than most other forms of marketing. When I have a new book release, as soon as I send my newsletter out announcing the release, I get a big spike in sales for the next few days, and it costs me about fifty dollars a month.

Sometimes authors feel trepidation about newsletters

if they aren't confident about what to include in their newsletter. There are two main components to a successful newsletter.

Reader engagement. Don't send out a newsletter only when you have a new release. This will feel "sales-y" to many of your readers and is a recipe for unsubscribes. Instead, you can have articles on where you are with the development of your work-in-progress, recommendations for other books in your genre, stories about what's going on in your non-author life (I recently made a cross-country move, and had a few articles about that), and any BookFunnel or StoryOrigin promos. Depending on your genre, you can share recipes, your favorite cosplay costumes, interesting trivia facts you've discovered in your research, or updates on your pets (popular with romance and cozy mystery readers).

Send it out regularly. I send my newsletter out every other week, except when I have a new release—then I'll send my newsletter out weekly. Most book marketing experts agree that you don't want to send newsletters less frequently than once a month or more frequently than once a week. Sending the newsletter on a pre-set day of the week is usually more effective too—my readers have come to expect my newsletter to hit their inbox every other Tuesday. (Although when I've sent a communication a day late, it's not a big deal.)

BUILDING A NEWSLETTER LIST: BOOKFUNNEL AND STORYORIGIN

These two websites are relatively cheap; both work out to less than $15 per month if you pay annually.

The idea behind these websites is to use other authors to promote your books (and for you to promote other authors' books).

This is done by signing your book up for a promotion in your genre. Each promotion on BookFunnel and StoryOrigin contain many books. All the authors who sign up agree to send a link to that promotion to their newsletter lists. There are different requirements for the promotions: some want books that are only in Amazon's KU program (which requires you to be exclusive to Amazon with your ebooks); some are for book sales; some are for short stories; some are for samples; some require all authors to have a minimum number of people on their mailing list; some will take newbie authors. (Many authors who organize these promos remember back to the days they had two people on their mailing list, and want to help others out too!)

When the newsletter readers of all the different authors click on the promo link in the authors' newsletters—including yours—they go to a promo page with all the book covers in the promo showing. A reader clicks on an interesting book cover and (usually) can download that book for free by simply signing up to that author's newsletter. If you're in a BookFunnel or StoryOrigin promo with 30 authors, you'll be offering your free book to 29 other sets of newsletter subscribers—and hopefully signing up many of them to your own newsletter.

Some authors have told me that they hate getting author newsletters on a regular basis and only want notifications of new releases, so that's all they do. There are two problems with this mindset: 1) many people *want* to engage with you as an author, and are less likely to buy if they're not engaged; and 2) if you don't send your newsletter out on a regular basis, it doesn't get a chance to engage with readers and your newsletter will more likely to end up in your subscribers' spam folders.

I was once one of those authors who had only two people on my mailing list. As soon as I published my second book, I joined BookFunnel and gave away my first book for free in a bunch of promotions. I required people to subscribe to my newsletter in order to get my free first book, and in six weeks, I went from a handful of subscribers to 1,600. That was four years ago, and my subscriber list has now grown to more than 7,000.

There is a debate among indie author marketing experts whether offering a full book for free in BookFunnel and StoryOrigin promos is wise; these experts instead recommend an exclusive piece (often a short story) in exchange for an email address. In the pricing discussion later in the book, I'll go into the pros and cons in more detail. (Both BookFunnel and StoryOrigin offer lots of different services for authors, and all the services center around either delivering your books to readers or promoting your books to readers.)

OTHER WAYS TO ATTRACT NEWSLETTER SUBSCRIBERS

In addition to BookFunnel and StoryOrigin promos, you can create your own website and offer a free short story, map of your world, background dossier on your spy character, or first novel in trade for the reader signing up to your newsletter. (I do this with a free short story; fulfillment of the short story and management of the subscription is done through BookFunnel.) Some authors offer a link following the last paragraph of their ebook to a newsletter subscription page where the reader can download an epilogue or a side story that's only available to newsletter subscribers.

WHAT IF YOU HATE MAKING NEWSLETTERS?

I have found that although creating and sending a newsletter on a regular basis is proven as an effective vehicle for sales, many authors hate doing it. I have author friends who don't know what to put in their newsletter, feel like they're being gross when they send out their newsletter, procrastinate creating their newsletter, and feel like they shouldn't say anything unless they have a new release.

If you're one of these anti-newsletter authors, I

believe a mindset change is in order. Many readers enjoy engaging with authors. If none of the above ideas for reader engagement are meaningful to you, it might be a "fake it until you make it" situation: write short articles about books, discuss research you've done, or simply link to low-cost books in your genre. You don't have to spill any information about your personal life, but it is important that some of your newsletter subscribers look forward to getting that communication from you—they'll be the ones who buy the day you release your next book.

THE COST OF EMAIL NEWSLETTERS

The cost of putting out newsletters might be your biggest expense. The two most common newsletter tools that authors use, MailChimp and MailerLite, cost more than $50 per month for many authors who have more than one or two thousand subscribers—and you'll need a mailing list that size if you want to make $1,000 a month. There are many other options for your email newsletters that are far cheaper, especially if you have programming experience. Some of the cheaper options, however, have lower deliverability rates, meaning that your newsletter might get filtered out by your subscribers' email servers before it ever gets to their inboxes. Having a good quality email marketing tool, however, is often essential to building a successful author business.

If you still are unsure about newsletters, Tammi

Labrecque's book *Newsletter Ninja* has many other tips, tricks, and best practices for making your newsletter work for you. Many authors find her advice tremendously helpful. (She runs a popular and active Facebook group on the subject as well.)

ADVERTISING IN PAID PROMO NEWSLETTERS

I've built most of my sales around **paid promo newsletters**. Unlike your author newsletter, paid promo newsletters are run by for-profit companies that are constantly attracting readers to subscribe. Authors (like you and me) will pay money to advertise our book, which is usually offered for free, 99¢, or at a significant discount, to all the subscribers of their newsletter. Well-known paid promo newsletters include BookBub, Freebooksy, eReader News Today, Fussy Librarian, and RobinReads—and there are dozens more.

If you write in a series, having a free first-in-series as your Entry Point Novel is what you'll want to promote. If you're a standalone author, paid promo newsletters *might* work for you for reduced-cost books for your Entry Point Novel. There are specific paid promo newsletters that specialize in higher-cost paid books as well, such as Early Bird Books.

Some of these paid promo newsletters go to readers of all categories, while others go only to readers who have asked for books in a particular genre. In my experience, the companies that provide genre-based newsletters perform better. (This applies to companies that offer many different genres, but require readers to sign up for the genres they want, as well as companies that offer only books in one or two genres.)

Book marketing experts Dave Chesson (with his Kindlepreneur website) and David Gaughran (with his eponymous website) have compiled lists of paid promo newsletters that have proven to be effective for authors. Their lists are updated frequently, and they both recommend the popular newsletters mentioned above.

In my experience, repeating promos to the same book leads to a decreasing number of downloads with each promo. For this reason, I don't repeat promos any more frequently than once every six months. With one $30 promo newsletter, I got 500 downloads the first time, 250 downloads six months after that, and 180 six months after that.

Some promo newsletters are free or low-cost (under $15) and other similar free promos promise that your Entry Point Novel will get included in a list on a website or through social media promotion. In my experience, running a promotion to my Entry Point Novel with these free or low-cost promotions resulted in 20 to 50 downloads.

The next tier of paid promo newsletters costs about $20 to $35. The first time I ran promos on these newsletters, I received 200 to 400 downloads, but when I re-ran them six months later, the downloads went down to 50 to 100.

There's generally a positive bump in quality to the next tier: paid promo newsletters that are $40-$60, including eReader News Today. You can find several genre-specific newsletters in this tier as well. I consistently get 250 to 750 downloads every time I run them.

The most effective newsletters that I run are in the next tier:.

- **Freebooksy** and **Fussy Librarian** are $25 to $150 (depending on genre and the options you choose).
- **BookBub Featured Deals** are significantly more expensive, and much harder to be accepted into. I've gotten rejected many times, and only accepted three times. I was lucky enough to get my Entry Point Novel accepted to a BookBub Featured Deal in their Crime Fiction newsletter, which goes to over three million readers. (This was *after* I was making $1,000 a month, and I firmly believe that my slow-and-steady ramp up to moderate success was part of the reason I was chosen.)

Be aware that you may have very different experiences with these newsletters. I've heard authors have great success with BookGorilla and BookRaid, but I've had very poor numbers with them. Other authors *hate* BooksButterfly, but their promos have always done well for me. Some newsletter will only promote books on Amazon, while others will promote wide books too; choose accordingly if you're in KU or if you're wide.

If you have multiple series—and multiple Entry Point Novels—you can increase the number of newsletter promos you can run. If you can be successful promoting multiple books in multiple series, it can get you to $1,000 a month quickly.

ADVERTISING ON FACEBOOK, AMAZON, AND BOOKBUB

If you are making less than $1,000 a month, I wouldn't recommend trying your hand at advertising unless you have additional money that you'd like to invest in your business. As of this writing, the "big three" of indie book advertising are Amazon, Facebook, and BookBub ads, and all three of them usually require significant experimentation and tweaking before you get those ads to break even, and even more before they turn a profit. Even successful authors who find their ads are profitable can spend 75% of what their ads bring in on the ads themselves. I spent six months tweaking my Facebook ads before I got a single one of them to perform well. (More than two years later, I'm still running the same ad!) I spent longer than that fiddling with Amazon and BookBub ads, but so far I have not figured out how to make those ads successful; I have yet to turn a significant profit. When you're making money, you can look into Amazon, Facebook, and BookBub ads—there are books from marketing experts like M.D. Cooper, Bryan Cohen, and David Gaughran as well as online classes dedicated to making these ads work for you.

CHAPTER 13
FIGURING OUT WHICH PROMOTIONS WORK

IF YOU HAVE SET up your website, newsletter, StoryOrigin/BookFunnel, and newsletter promos, you're ready to run your promos and analyze the results. As much as I hate math, I wasn't looking forward to the analysis of this—but I hate wasting money more than I hate math. I had to break out a spreadsheet to figure this next part out.

SEPARATE YOUR PROMOTIONS

When you run promotions and ads, you aren't always able to separate which promo or ad has resulted in which downloads. Some marketing experts say that you want to "stack" your promotions and ads, because if those sales all come on the same day, it can activate the mysterious algorithms at book retailer sites, putting your book in front of more readers—although I don't think that's been proven. My concern: if I stack promos, I can't see which promos result in which downloads. (Very few of the promo newsletters will provide information on their results.)

However, if you isolate your promos by spacing them out at least three or four days apart, you can get at least a rough idea of how many downloads have resulted from each of those promos. Promo newsletters will perform the most strongly the day of the promo, then will provide a much smaller bump on day two, and an even smaller bump on day three. One of my best promos a couple of years ago netted me about 500 downloads on day one, 100 on day two, and 50 on day three.

If you have the money for Facebook or Amazon ads, you can track your own reporting for ads too. Fortunately, ads are better—not great, but better—at reporting.

You can get your book download and purchase data from a few different places. All the book retailers and ebook aggregators provide their own reporting, but going to each of them and entering the data into a spreadsheet can be time-consuming and tedious (especially when a couple of those sites make you dig for the data). I like third-party reporting tools like ScribeCount or BookReport to centralize reporting (though they're not perfect, they make it far easier and save me hours of time every month). From those reports, you can get the number of downloads of your free first-in-series and the number of sales of your second book in the series on a day-by-day basis, and from those numbers, you can get the data you need to make decisions regarding your author business to get to $1,000 a month.

For example, if you have 1,000 downloads of Book 1 and 30 purchases of Book 2, you have a 3% readthrough rate to Book 2.

One note: It's a guessing game to figure out when to calculate readthrough, because you have readers who will burn through Book 1 in five hours and buy Book 2 the same day, and others who will take a month—or even a year—to get through Book 1. Two weeks is what some experts use, though others will say 30 or even 60 days. Romance readers have a reputation for being voracious, with many of them reading two or three books a day. For romance authors, a two-week cycle may provide more accurate reporting numbers than that cycle would for an epic fantasy author.

You can also get the readthrough rate from Book 2 to Book 3, three to four... and so forth. In the whole series, you can then calculate how much money you can make off each download.

For example, let's say you have a four-book series. You are promoting your Entry Point Novel, and you've decided to make it free. You buy a slot in a paid promo newsletter, then you get the results of your sales in two weeks (or 30 days, or whatever you decide):

- Entry Point Novel (Book 1): 1,000 downloads
- Book 2: 50 purchases at $4.99 (5% readthrough with a royalty of $3.50 each, or $175)

- Book 3: 30 purchases at $4.99 ($105)
- Book 4: 25 purchases at $4.99 ($87.50)

Your 1,000 downloads have resulted in sales of $367.50. So each download makes you about $0.37. If you're paying more than that per download, you're not making any money.

There are three "levers" to pull in order to change the amount of revenue per download.

- Modifying your Entry Point Novel (to increase the readthrough)
- Altering the price of the books
- Adding to the number of books in the series

Treating your Entry Point Novel like "your best advertisement ever" may lead you to modify the book to make the intro more grabby, to make the characters more intriguing, to heighten the conflict, to tighten up the pacing—in short, to do everything you can to get readers hungrily turning those pages and ordering Book 2. As mentioned before, my editor insisted that I do this with my Entry Point Novel to increase my readthrough.

Another thing I did to increase my readthrough was include the first few chapters of my Book 2 immediately following the last chapter of my Entry Point Novel—with a link to buy Book 2 after the final paragraph of the preview.

In addition, about a month after making my Entry

Point Novel free on all platforms, I took the advice of David Gaughran and *lowered* the price of Book 2 to $2.99 from $4.99. At the time, I had about a 3.5% readthrough from Book 1 to Book 2, and a 67% readthrough from Book 2 to Book 3. I was skeptical about the change; my royalties on the $4.99 Book 2 was about $3.40, but royalties on a $2.99 Book 2 would be about $2.04. My sales of that second book would have to jump 60% to break even—and I was afraid the readthrough percentage to Book 3 would plummet.

But David Gaughran is very experienced in the indie author world, so I followed his advice. And lo and behold —my readthrough to Book 2 *tripled*. For a couple of months, my readthrough from my free Entry Point Novel to Book 2 was almost 10%—and my readthrough to Book 3 only fell from 67% to 66%—the 1% difference isn't even statistically significant. Not only was I making three times what I'd made before on Books 3 through 5, I was also significantly raising my revenue per download. Because my readthrough was making me nearly $1 per download, I could afford to buy promos in newsletters that had lost me money before.

A few months after I made my Entry Point Novel free, I released Book 6 in the series, which again lifted my overall revenue-per-download. (I've since released Books 7 and 8, as well as two novellas that take place between two of the other books.) Because my readthrough to my later books is over 90%, I've now calculated that I'm making almost $2 for every free Entry Point Novel that gets downloaded. Some authors—like Mark Dawson, who has over 20 books in his main series—make several times that.

I want to make money with my books. I know that I can spend almost $1 to get a download of my Entry Point Novel in order to double my investment. If you're starting with three or four books, you need to find out your "break even" point for each download of your Entry Point Novel and commit to spending less than that to get a download.

NOISE IN THE DATA

I track my sales numbers for each day, because when a promotion runs, I want to know how many downloads I get. However, that doesn't really tell me how effective the promotion is. That would require knowing which of the downloads go on to purchase Book 2, and the e-retailers and promo newsletter companies don't break down the information like that.

So it's possible that one of my newsletters that gets 1,000 downloads only results in two or three sales of Book 2, whereas another that only gets 50 downloads of Book 1 gets 50 downloads of Book 2. It wouldn't be accurate to assume that all readers targeted with all these different promo newsletters have the same reading and purchasing habits.

Also, after I was making decent money every month, I started experimenting with advertising. As a result, I keep an effective Facebook ad running constantly. When

I'm not running any promos, I usually get between 30 and 50 downloads of Book 1 every day (though occasionally it's higher or lower—I've had some days when I only get 10 downloads, and some where I get 100), and I assume that the Facebook ad is responsible for most of that. (Not to take you down a rabbit hole, but there are ways that you can track *some* of the purchases made from Facebook ads, but not with most e-retailers—and it's complicated, anyway. I don't do it; maybe I should.)

Unfortunately, I'm currently unable to tell if the day I run a promo is a good Facebook ad day or a bad Facebook ad day. The variance is a couple of dozen book downloads, so if I run the inexpensive ads that may only net me 20 or 30 downloads (which, at $15, would still be quite profitable, percentage-wise), I'm often unable to tell if it *really* netted me 20 or 30 downloads, or if it completely failed and I got zero downloads from it. (I've experimented with many of these newsletter promos, and I've sometimes had a *lower* number of Book 1 downloads on a promo day than the day before when I wasn't running the promo—it's a bummer, but at least I know to avoid that promo in the future.)

Some of the newsletter promos don't allow you to pick your date, either, so there are times when the promo runs on a day when I've already got another promo running. (And if you decide to follow some of the experts' advice and stack your promos, you may not know which promos are effective—but if you believe that stacking the promos juices the retailer algorithms to provide more downloads anyway, you may not care if you can get data from each promo individually.)

MAKING DECISIONS WITH INCOMPLETE INFORMATION

Before the advent of digital marketing and audience tracking, there was a common adage in the marketing world: **"Half my advertising spend is wasted; the trouble is, I don't know which half."** This quote has been attributed to both John Wanamaker (a retail leader in the U.S.) and Lord Leverhulme (an industrialist in the U.K.). Data tracking has, thankfully, improved since the early 20th century when this phrase was coined, but the data still isn't perfect. The information available to indie authors doesn't match everything authors need to know to make business decisions.

In short, you'll need to make decisions based on incomplete information.

It's very similar to fixing the problem of why a book or book series isn't selling. With my aforementioned romance series, I had what experts told me was a great title, a fantastic cover, and a terrific concept that would appeal to a vastly underserved market. The books were well-written, the heat level was clear from the covers and the blurb. It was only when I dug into reader reactions—not my *early readers*, who felt like they had an obligation to read farther than the first chapter—did I discover that there were major problems with the whole concept of the series. And while I'm pretty sure that's the issue, there's really no way to be 100% positive. I made a business decision to stop all promotion of that book series because fixing those major problems would be too much work to be worth it. However, if I'm wrong, and a small tweak to the cover or a retitling of the series or a rewrite of the first chapter of the Entry Point Novel of that series would make the series sell, I've made another error. With the information available to me, however, setting my romance series aside and focusing on my mysteries was, I believe, the right decision for me.

Company leaders must make difficult decisions based on incomplete information all the time; indie author businesses are no different. You can get as informed as possible in a reasonable time frame, but you'll need to make some painful decisions at some point in your author career, and you won't have as much data as you want.

CHAPTER 14

PRICING: STRATEGY AND BALANCE

YOU WILL HAVE to determine what price to charge for each of your published books, whether you're on KU or not, and the prices you charge can dramatically alter the amount of money you make.

MY PRICING STRATEGY

Offering a free first-in-series (FFIS), like I do, has worked for me. (As with everything in the indie author world, what works for many authors may not work for you.)

As I mentioned earlier, when I first offered my Entry Point Novel for free, I sold Books 2 through 5 at $4.99 each. I was seeing a readthrough from Book 1 to Book 2 at about 3.5%. I took book marketing expert David Gaughran's advice and lowered the cost of Book 2 from $4.99 to $2.99. I tripled my readthrough, and I made more money after the price drop.

So my pricing strategy is offering Book 1 for free,

Book 2 for a reduced price, and full price on the rest of the series. This is my "default pricing."

PRICING HIGH OR LOW

Reducing the price on your books doesn't always boost your sales—and even if it does, it may not maximize your income. Sometimes you can raise your price and not significantly affect the number of units sold. I know several authors who raised the price of their books from $4.99 to $6.99 with only a 5% or 10% reduction in the number of units sold. (My theory is that a certain kind of reader will purchase a book they think they'll like, and it will have to get quite expensive before those readers *won't* buy the next book in the series.)

In the consumer products market, there are some products that will sell more at higher price points because of their *perceived value*. Many luxury brands sell much better at higher prices than at lower prices, because some consumers want to pay for the perceived quality (or for the designer name). Non-fiction titles—especially business-related books—tend to be given more weight if they're priced somewhat higher. A 99¢ self-help book may feel to readers as if it's cheap because its advice isn't effective. As a result, non-fiction readers are considered significantly less price-sensitive than fiction readers.

While price sensitivity is much more common in fiction, much depends on genre and reader expectations. There are quite a few readers who don't mind spending

$10 (or more) for a quality fiction ebook that they are confident they'll like. But this will vary for every author out there. Unfortunately, there's no real way to determine what your best price point is without experimenting. If you already have an established reader base, it might be hard for them to accept a price increase for your next release—but you'll never know if you don't try.

Be aware, too, that some e-retailers take a larger cut of sales than others. It's fairly common for retailers to give you 35% of the sale price of ebooks listed under $2.99, and 65-70% of ebooks $2.99 and up. Amazon, the most popular retailer, lowers the author's share back to 35% for ebooks over $9.99, whereas most other retailers keep $9.99+ ebooks at 65-70%.

SELLING AT 99¢

If your goal is to get to $1,000 a month, be aware that because most retailers only give you 35% of a book sold at 99¢ (about 34¢) but 70% of a book sold at $2.99 (about $2.09, though some retailers charge a few cents for delivery too), it will take six sales of your 99¢ ebook to get you the same amount of money you'd make with one sale at $2.99.

Sometimes this makes sense: 99¢ is a more attractive price point, and if you believe that people will read through to your next books in significant numbers, then you may want to offer your book—perhaps for a promotional period, and in combination with promo newsletters

—for 99¢. Getting the book in the hands of more readers might be worth it—but keep track of your numbers in the 30 days after you drop the price to 99¢ to see if that's the case.

I recently dropped the price of my Book 2 from $2.99 to 99¢/99p for a promotion that I ran using some of those promo newsletters I've mentioned in previous chapters. On average, I sold about five to six times the number of Book 2s that I usually sell during the promo period, so I broke even on sales. However, the promos cost me about $200, and I was hoping that the readthrough to the rest of the series would pay for the promos (and then some). My unit sales for the next 30 days, however, didn't bump up all that much—about 5%. That's roughly enough to break even on the promo newsletter cost, but obviously not as successful as I hoped. There are other factors at play here, too: the 99¢ promo was for Book 2 in the series, and readthrough might not be as linear as a Book 1 offering would be; having Book 1 in the same series for free might be affecting readthrough as well. In addition, 30 days might not be enough time to assess the success of this promo. I may end up running this type of promo again: it didn't lose money, and it may have a long tail, making me significant money over the next several months.

SELLING FOR FREE

I've mentioned free first-in-series (FFIS) quite a bit. If you go onto your KDP dashboard on Amazon, however, you will discover that you cannot make any of the books you sell free—in fact, you can't sell any ebook for under 99¢. So how do you do it?

For KU authors, it's straightforward: you can make your book free for five days out of every 90-day KDP Select period. You'll have to time all your FFIS promotions on those five days, but many KU authors do this successfully.

For wide authors, it's trickier. First, *all* other large ebook retailers allow you to make any book in your catalog free. The first thing you'll have to do is go onto all your e-retailer and aggregator dashboards and change the price to $0.00. Once the price change has been implemented—and make sure it's implemented in all regions, not just your country—Amazon might "price match" that title to free automatically.

If, after a week, they have not made the book free, you'll have to contact Amazon to request a "price match" (through the KDP help tools; the methods for doing this change all the time). When I did this, I was able to request a call from an Amazon agent who then required all the URLs for four different stores (and in multiple countries) to show that my book was free everywhere else. This took about three hours for me, and the agent told me the price would be matched within 72 hours (although it was closer to 24 hours). If you do this, it's a huge pain in the neck, but if you are prepared with the URLs, if you double-check the pricing before you call, and if you are kind, patient, and helpful to the agent, you will likely get price-matched to free in a timely manner.

WHEN TO GO FREE

If you only have one book, experts don't recommend going free. In order to give something away, you need to get something in return.

If you have four or more books in your series, what you get in return for a FFIS that you promote using newsletter promos is a wider audience who will buy Book 2—and hopefully the rest of the series.

If you have one or two books in your series, leaving Book 1 (your Entry Point Novel) for sale on the e-retailer sites (perhaps at $2.99-$4.99) will give you the ability to make some money on those. Beginning authors often wonder if they can make their ebook free on just one retailer. Unfortunately, all of the "terms of service" (TOS) documents for the e-retailers specify that you cannot sell your book for a lower price on any other e-retailer's site.

If you then put your Entry Point Novel in Book-Funnel or StoryOrigin promos and give it away for free (wide authors only—and you're not violating the TOS because BookFunnel and StoryOrigin aren't book retailers), you are trading your book for an email address—and hopefully a percentage of those newsletter subscribers will purchase future releases.

Many book experts do *not* recommend this. Instead,

the experts encourage an *exclusive* prequel, a short story, a side journey, or another piece of writing (often called a "reader magnet") that is only offered in exchange for an email address. (This is often done on your author website instead of or in addition to BookFunnel or StoryOrigin.) These experts don't want authors to cannibalize their sales, and they also believe that the exclusivity will attract a higher quality of reader to your email list.

I disagree with this. A short reader magnet has worked for many authors, but in my experience, the number of people who want to read a full-length novel is much, much higher than the number of people who want a short story or a side quest. I believe that if you just offer a short reader magnet, you'll be excluding many readers who would buy your books if they were to start with a full-length novel. However, there is a risk of getting more "freebie-seekers" on your mailing list, which can be annoying (and eventually can cost more).

Again, every author's journey is different.

SELLING FOR DIFFERENT PRICES ACROSS DIFFERENT STORES

As mentioned above, all the TOS agreements from all the retailers specify that you cannot offer your book for a lower price on any other retailer. Even if you think that readers on one store will pay $6.99 for your book, but on another they won't pay more than $2.99, you cannot offer your book for different prices.

However, several retailers offer *coupon codes*. You can provide interested readers with coupon codes so that when they purchase your book, they pay $2.99 instead of $6.99. (Most retailers offer percent-off codes, not price-specific codes, but the idea is the same.)

This applies to books above $9.99 as well; as mentioned previously, Amazon only gives you 35% of the sales price of books with a list price above $9.99, whereas most other retailers give you 65-70%. If you have a box set containing five of your books (retailers usually prefer the terms "omnibus" or "collection" rather than "box set"), you can't offer your collection for $15 on Kobo or Barnes & Noble and $30 on Amazon (even though you would be receiving the same amount of royalty payment on each sale).

There are a few pricing tactics that indie authors have used to combat the $9.99 Amazon cap.

- For wide authors, some make collections of their ebooks available only on those retailers who keep the higher percentages.
- For KU authors, some make omnibus or collections available at a very inflated price (for example, if buying the books separately cost $20 total, they'll sell the collection at $30 or $40). This depresses the number of sales at 35%, but can raise the number of KU page reads (especially for value-minded KU

readers who see that they can get a $30 or $40 book for "free").
- Many authors choose to cap the prices for all their books (including their collections) at $9.99—or only offer smaller collections (for example, threebook collections) on Amazon, while making larger, more expensive collections available on other stores.
- Some authors who have written very long novels—200,000 words or longer—sometimes will split the book into a trilogy to sell it on Amazon. Three 70,000-word novels sold at $4.99 will be roughly equivalent to a 210,000-word novel sold at $14.99.

FIGURING OUT YOUR PRICE

Once all the pricing rules, guidelines, and regulations are in your head, how do you figure out what to sell for?

Take a look at other books in the genre you're writing. Traditionally published ebooks often sell for over $10, but for the indie authors in your genre, what are they doing? How long are their books, and what are their price points? How are those books selling? (You can see the sales ranking on many e-retailer sites.)

Unless you have a compelling reason to do otherwise, duplicate the pricing model that successful authors have used in your genre. Remember, it's about matching reader expectations, not using price as a differentiator to your books (unless it's the Book 1 you're using as your advertisement). Don't be afraid to experiment with pricing longer (or higher-quality) books higher than shorter or lower-quality books.

If you have a series, consider pricing your books to encourage readers to buy the whole series. For me, that's a free first-in-series (FFIS), a $2.99 Book 2, and full-price ($4.99) books for the rest of the series. If you have stand-alone novels in addition to a series, be aware that most of your readers will only consider purchasing those *after* going through your series, so price accordingly. After finishing a standalone novel, there's nowhere else for your reader to go that is as compelling as the next book in a series.

CHAPTER 15
STARTING WITH NO MONEY

ONE OF THE great things about starting an author business is that you need significantly less capital than almost every other business—as mentioned in Chapter 3, with manuscript and editing costs of less than $2,000 and a monthly marketing spend of $200, you can be on your way.

But many authors find themselves with no money to spend at all. They may have a computer and internet access, and that's it. Can you still start an author business with no money invested up front?

Yes—but you'll need to go into this with your eyes open. You'll be much less likely to create a compelling Entry Point Novel, you'll have far fewer tools at your disposal, and you'll expend a lot more effort to make up for the lack of tools. You'll often have to give just as much of your time, effort, and attention to other writers as you get in return.

- **Manuscript:** There's no way around this: you will need a computer and writing software. Maybe you can use a laptop you have from work, maybe your local library is an option, or maybe you can beg an old PC from a relative. Email accounts are free, and so is Google Docs.
- **Editing**: If you can't pay for editing, the next best thing is to find a critique group. There are groups all over the world that meet in person, as well as dozens who meet online. You can use social media or web searches to find many of these groups. You'll need to pay close attention to those critique group members who are familiar with the genre you're writing in, as well as those members who are truly helpful with their comments compared to those who criticize or praise needlessly. You may need to invest a lot of time in finding critique groups (or a critique partner) who is effective at improving your manuscript. You should also expect lower quality editing; critique partners won't have the time or effort to expend on the truly helpful analysis that might significantly improve your book. This is a two-way street: you will have to be the kind of critical voice that you'd want to hear.

- **Proofreading**: You may know local members of the Grammar Police who are more than happy to attack your manuscript with a red pen to find dangling modifiers and misused commas. If you find such a person, refer them to *The Chicago Manual of Style* (or the relevant style guide from your country) before you set them loose on your manuscript. Before you publish, read the book out loud; you'll find many typos, repeated words, and other easily fixable errors.
- **Interior design of ebook and print book:** Calibre and Kindle Create are free, so creating the ebook interior can be a no-cost exercise. Draft2Digital and Reedsy both have free tools for print interiors you can use in exchange for signing up on their websites (which does not require any money to exchange hands). Their tools are fussy, but if you format your Google Doc properly, it's doable.
- **Cover design:** If you have a little money, you might be able to use GetCovers or find a cheap artist on Fiverr. If you have the time and patience to sit through some YouTube tutorials on creating your own covers, you can use free software tools from Canva or other websites to do it yourself. Be especially aware

of the expected cover designs in your genre if you go this route, as this is often the most difficult task for authors to do themselves and look professional. Be cautious of websites that promise free artwork (or designers that promise too-cheap-to-be-true covers): often, those images are copyrighted and cannot be used for cover art, despite what the website says.

- **Blurb**: Look at the other blurbs of successful books in your genre: most of them are not plot summaries, but rather they are like advertising copy, compelling the reader to buy the book to answer interesting questions. Phoebe Ravencraft and Bryan Cohen's book on fiction blurbs is an excellent introduction to the art of crafting great blurbs that get customers to buy.
- **Logistics:** If you can't afford to buy your own ISBNs, all the online book retailers will supply ISBNs for free. Amazon and Barnes & Noble will also supply free ISBNs for your print books.
- **Mailing list and newsletter**: Many email offerings allow a certain number of recipients for free before they start to charge a monthly fee. MailerLite, EmailOctopus, and others have free tiers. This can get you off the ground—and by the time you have

enough subscribers to require payment, you'll hopefully be making enough money to cover the monthly charge.
- **Getting your book out there**: While they may not move the needle much, free book promotion options, like SnicksList, are available. In addition, social media accounts are generally free: getting the word out on Facebook, Twitter, Instagram, TikTok, and other platforms requires effort and time, but no money. Don't promote your book on writing groups; that's a great way to get kicked out of those groups. Instead, create your own pages and try to connect with people in reader groups before you try to sell your book. This can be slow and it requires a lot of nuanced effort to get right, but some people have done it. A big downside to this is that you don't own the list of people who engage with you; if you get kicked off Instagram or Facebook, you've lost that whole avenue to engage people. (Try to get them to sign up for your mailing list, which you *do* own.)
- **Consider bartering**. Is there part of the self-publishing process that you do particularly well? Maybe you have a great eye for proofreading, or maybe you have a background in graphic design. Consider

offering your services to other self-published authors in exchange for what *they* are good at. But don't oversell your services; if you're no good at cover art, don't say you are just to get someone else to proofread your book. The indie author world is fairly insular, and word gets around fast.

- **Learn the limitations of your no-spend strategy.** Editing, cover design, and marketing are three areas where it's difficult to do things yourself. Keep your eyes open—and check your ego—to be open to ways to improve. You'll also need to be honest with yourself about where you need the most help when you *do* have money to spend.
- **Have a plan to transition away from your no-spend strategy**. How much money will you need to make every month before you can start investing some of that money back into your business? While you may find that some aspects of your cost-saving plan are working well, other areas may need the keen eye of a professional. Tools like BookFunnel are inexpensive and needed, so the first couple of hundred dollars you make should go toward those types of tools if possible.
- **Give back**. My cover designer worked for a bottle of bourbon for a long time, but once I

started making enough money, I paid him in actual currency. So don't take advantage of those people who have donated their time and expertise to you; when you are at a point when you are making enough money, pay them what they're worth. And never forget that you started with a no-money plan, so when others come to you for your expertise—because you *will* gain expertise through this experience—that you take them under your wing just as others did with you.

PART THREE
PUTTING IT ALL TOGETHER

CHAPTER 16
PRIORITIZE

FOR AN AUTHOR STARTING OUT—OR who has several books, but hasn't gotten over the hump of $1,000 a month—this all can feel overwhelming. What do you do first—and how do you figure out how to prioritize everything?

FOCUS ON THE PRODUCT FIRST

Your books are what you sell, and without a quality product, the marketing will be less efficient—or even ineffective. But, as mentioned earlier, it's not just about a well-written book. It's about meeting your audience's expectations, and that means writing a book that you can effectively connect to your reading audience.

Yes, the books must look and feel professional—indistinguishable from traditionally published books—but if you want to have positive cash flow as an author, you must know, understand, and internalize how you're going to get readers to buy the books you have for sale.

And this starts with the kind of products you're going to produce. So prioritize getting "yes" answers to the following questions:

- Will your books be easy to categorize?
- Will your books be easy to find on the retailers' websites?
- Will each cover lure readers to click on it when the thumbnail is shown alongside twenty other books?
- Once the readers start reading your Entry Point Novel, will they understand what they're getting into? Will they be treated to the same kind of book they expected to read when they downloaded or purchased it?
- Will readers be compelled to follow the characters through multiple journeys?
- Will readers find it easy to find and purchase the next book you've written?

As indie authors, writing a series that treats the entry point as an advertisement for the rest of your books is a proven route to success. In that entry point, you need to (figuratively) make a promise to your readers that they will get an enjoyable book following characters they love (or love to hate, or whatever)—just like the book (or the "advertisement") they just read.

These questions are more important than anything else, because getting "yes" answers means that when someone picks up your Entry Point Novel, you have maximized the chance that they will make an actual purchase of your next book.

If that chance is only 1%, you will have trouble making money from your promotions. If that chance is 10%, you will have a much better chance of making (and exceeding) that $1,000-a-month goal.

Getting your first book—your "advertisement"—and the rest of your products in place will require monetary investment in editing, cover design, interior layout, and some basic marketing and readership-building tools like an email newsletter tool, a book distribution and promotion subscription (BookFunnel and/or StoryOrigin) and a website. Not many authors can learn to do these on their own at a professional level, but if you feel that you're the exception, you'll have to put in the time and effort to get the instruction to do it, often through paid classes or books.

Don't prioritize awards, bestseller lists, or traditional advertising. Those methods have their place, but usually *after* you're making more than $1,000 a month.

Most importantly, keep your goal in mind whenever you have a decision to make about your author business. It's true that advertising on Amazon, Facebook, and BookBub has worked for many authors, but if it's not the right time—or if it's too much money—then it won't support your goal of making $1,000 a month. Just because something is important to do doesn't mean it's the right thing for *you* to do at this stage of your career.

CHAPTER 17
PLAN AND EXECUTE

AFTER YOU BELIEVE your Entry Point Novel is where it needs to be, and now that you're familiar with the different facets of marketing, it's time to choose the options you're going to execute, prioritize their importance, and put them into a plan.

BALANCING MARKETING AND WRITING

Writers can get overwhelmed with balancing the needs of their author business with the needs of their writing production. While promotions and marketing strategy are important, writing more books is also crucial to the long-term success of your author business—and having long series means that you will make more money when your promotions are successful.

While successful time management looks different for each person, many indie author marketing experts recommend carving out time for both writing and marketing as part of your writing week. Some people feel more creative in the morning, so they use time before work to write; when they are more tired after work, they use that time to set up promotions and write email newsletters. Your journey will be very different than everyone else when it comes to this, particularly if you are raising small children or are a caregiver for a parent. My recommendation is to pay attention to the times and situations in which you are most effective at both writing and the marketing work you need to do, and to try to adjust your schedule accordingly.

At the beginning of your author journey, you'll find yourself inundated with information, which can be overwhelming. Don't try to do everything at once. Be aware that burnout is not only a "real thing," but has derailed many author careers. While you may be impatient to hit $1,000 a month, you'll find yourself with a much longer timeline if you burn out.

GETTING STARTED WITH MARKETING: BOOKFUNNEL OR STORYORIGIN

Your initial marketing plan should focus on how you'll start your promotions to get that Entry Point Novel—the advertisement—into readers' hands. For me, I began my book marketing journey with BookFunnel promo newsletters, getting that first quality book—my best advertisement—to my audience.

Setting up BookFunnel or StoryOrigin to work for you is fairly straightforward, but time-consuming nonetheless. I recommend listening to those episodes of writing podcasts where representatives from both BookFunnel and StoryOrigin talk about tips and tricks, as well as the right mindset, to be successful using the sites. Sometimes those representatives promote their newest tools, which can be beyond the needs of beginning authors, but listening to the programs' creators and leaders talk about how best to use their products is very helpful.

I recommend that you start with either BookFunnel *or* StoryOrigin, but not both. You can select two or three promo newsletters rather than a list of a dozen or more. You can take a month to focus on building your website rather than trying to cram everything into your first week of marketing efforts.

You're also not superhuman, so don't think you have to be a wizard at everything. I am not good at WordPress, so I use a build-your-own-website tool (Wix, Squarespace, and Strikingly are some of the more popular options) and I buy my domain name through that company. Yes, it's a bit limiting, and yes, it's a little more expensive than if I did my own WordPress site, but it's worth saving the time and effort to focus on the other parts of my writing business where I *am* more effective and I can play to my strengths.

Once you know where you're going to start, jump in. It may be daunting, but with the mindset and the tools from this book, it will hopefully be easier—and you'll feel like you're on solid ground. You'll make mistakes and you'll learn from them. I'm still making mistakes—and the tools and terms change so rapidly that you'll *always* be learning.

CHAPTER 18
A SAMPLE TIMELINE TO GET TO $1,000 A MONTH

I MENTIONED EARLIER that I hate math, but in order to get to $1,000 a month, you'll need to calculate your income and expenses at a minimum, and ideally, your 30-day readthrough rate (although you may find a different number of days that works better for you).

Let's take an example of the execution of this plan. For this example, let's assume you have two novels published in a series, with a third on its way, and your first-in-series as your Entry Point Novel. (This example is very close to my experience—filtering out the detours I took with books that didn't work.) Many indie authors can release three or four books in 18 months—in fact, some write a book a month. Others, however, may only write a book a year. If you're a slower writer, you may need to lengthen this timeline.

To start with, I recommend you invest in BookFunnel (or StoryOrigin) at $100 per year, in an email program (free to start with under 1,000 users), but you only have five subscribers. You sell your Entry Point Novel for $2.99 and your second book for $4.99. Last month, you made about $50 in sales, which came mostly from friends, family members, and co-workers—but a few people found your book organically and bought your stuff.

MONTH 1

In Month 1, you add your Entry Point Novel to Book-Funnel and sign up for two BookFunnel promos, which you send (along with an article on how your Book 3 is coming along, and a review of a recent book in your genre) to your newsletter subscribers. The 20 other authors in your BookFunnel promo do the same, and, along with 500 downloads of your Entry Point Novel, you get 500 newsletter subscribers—and 25 purchases of Book 2 (a 5% readthrough rate). You've also added the pre-order link for Book 3 immediately following the last paragraph in Book 2, and you get 10 pre-orders of Book 3.

Congratulations! In addition to the $50 you made this month from $2.99 sales of your Entry Point Novel and Book 2 in your series (the same as last month), you made an additional $87.50 from the additional BookFunnel-fueled sales of Book 2 (at a customer price of $4.99, you get about $3.50)—putting you at $137.50 for the month, although the BookFunnel annual fee of $100 took a good chunk out of that.

MONTH 2

You sign up for another two BookFunnel promos and send those promos to your 505 newsletter subscribers. You also send a Book 3 teaser (maybe it's the first chapter, maybe it's a cover art reveal) in your newsletter, along with a link to pre-order. These promos are a little different than the ones you tried the first month, and they bring you 1,000 more readers of your Entry Point Novel, along with 50 purchases of Book 2 and another 20 pre-orders of Book 3. Your newsletter also gets you another 20 pre-orders of Book 3.

In addition to the $50 you made from organic sales, you've added $175 in Book 2 sales, putting you at $225 for the month.

MONTH 3

You sign up for another two BookFunnel promos, and you release Book 3—along with an announcement of your news release to your 1,505 subscribers. (You're now paying $40 a month for your email list.) You've also added the pre-order for Book 4 after the last paragraph of Book 3.

These two BookFunnel promos don't do as well as last month—you only get 400 new downloads and subscribers. But your Book 3 release (at the $4.99 price point, you get about $3.50) brings you 100 orders of Book 3 from those 1,905 subscribers in addition to the

50 pre-orders you got over the last two months. Your organic sales are up to $100, because that bump in sales increased your visibility on both the top sellers in your categories as well as rising in the ranks on your search terms. This happens on a couple of the e-retailer sites.

Don't forget about your 5% readthrough to Book 2 from your BookFunnel promos, either—and it looks like about two-thirds of those Book 2 readers are buying Book 3.

- $350 in Book 3 sales from your newsletter.
- $105 in Book 3 sales from your 50 pre-orders.
- $70 in Book 2 sales from your BookFunnel promos.
- $45 in Book 3 sales from your BookFunnel promos.
- $100 in organic sales.

You've hit $670 for the month, paying an extra $40 for your email marketing program (and your expenses for editing and cover design—so you're not really in the black just yet).

TROUBLESHOOTING: WHAT HAPPENS IF THIS ISN'T WORKING?

There are some genres that don't have many promos in BookFunnel and StoryOrigin, and you may need to lower your expectations (and realize that your build to $1,000 a month may take longer).

If you're in a popular genre, however, and you're not seeing positive results, look at where the disconnect is.

ARE YOU NOT GETTING DOWNLOADS ON YOUR ENTRY POINT NOVEL?

There are **three common problems** if you're not getting as many downloads as you expect.

1. Your **cover** is amateurish, out-of-genre, or otherwise not meeting your readers' expectations, so they're unclear about what kind of story you're offering.
2. The **book description** (or blurb) for your novel is not well-written or doesn't match with the genre or reader expectations.
3. You've **miscategorized** the book or the promos, and your book isn't matching the audience of those promos.

How do you fix this? Many social media platforms have book marketing groups, some of which may offer critiques from people who are well-versed in covers, book descriptions/blurbs, and book promos. At the very least, ask a brutally honest friend, co-worker, acquaintance, or stranger **who reads the genre you write** to give you feedback on the cover, blurb, and category. You may need to do some painful and time-consuming work, much like I had to do when I converted the *Murders of Substance* series to the *Woodhead & Becker Mysteries*.

ARE YOU GETTING DOWNLOADS, BUT NOT GETTING READTHROUGH TO BOOK 2?

There are a few possibilities for this problem.

1. Your book has **too many editing errors**. Whether it's glaring point-of-view shifts, a plethora of typos and spelling errors, or distracting formatting issues, these can prevent a reader from finishing a book. In some cases, you may have had your book edited by someone who isn't familiar enough with readers' expectations of your genre. An author friend of mine had their first mystery novel edited by an editor who had only done romance novels; their novel did not conform to mystery readers' expectations.
2. Your book doesn't have **characters** that readers want to root for. If your readers don't care about your main character, they won't finish your book. (Matt Bird has an excellent book called *The Secrets of Character: Writing a Hero Everyone Will Love* that provides some excellent tips for creating a protagonist that will resonate with readers.)

3. Your book doesn't have an engaging **narrative or storyline**. If your readers are bored, if they're not sure what the main character's goal is, or if they don't think the main character is the one driving the action forward, they may not finish. (Many experts have books, sites, blogposts, and classes on improving narrative; you may want to focus on some that are specific to the genre you write.)

4. Your book is **breaking one of the core rules** for the genre—and isn't able to get away with it. If you've written a romance novel that doesn't have a happily-ever-after ending, if your mystery novel doesn't have a compelling mystery at its core, or if your sci-fi novel is full of elves and swords instead of spaceships and aliens, you may be getting downloads, but readers may not want to read more books of yours.

How do you fix this? The first problem is easily addressed with more skilled editors and proofreaders. The rest of the problems are not easily fixable and may require a significant rewrite—or, like I did with my romance series, chucking it in the bin and focusing on another series.

MONTHS 4-8

If you find that what you're doing so far is working, great! At this point, perhaps you're working feverishly to finish Book 4 in the series, and adding promos from StoryOrigin in there as well ($70 for the year). Between BookFunnel and StoryOrigin, you're participating in three promos a month, netting you an average of 600 new readers of your Entry Point Novel a month—30 new Book 2 buyers and 20 new Book 3 buyers. You've got nearly 6,000 people in your email list now, and your organic sales are hitting an average of $150 every month.

- $150 in organic sales.
- $175 in Book 2 and Book 3 sales from BookFunnel and StoryOrigin.

This adds up to $325 per month total—not $1,000, but over six times what you were selling only eight months ago.

MONTH 9

You release Book 4—and it's your most successful yet. Between the spike in sales when your newsletter announcement goes out and your pre-order fulfillment, you sell 200 copies of Book 4 at $4.99 ($3.50 in your pocket). You also have the pre-order for Book 5 at the end of Book 4, and you get 50 pre-orders.

You continue with BookFunnel and StoryOrigin, getting another 600 downloads and email addresses. Not only do you get your normal 30 Book 2 sales and 20 Book 3 sales, but you also get 18 Book 4 sales.

Your organic sales bump up again, this time to $200.

- $200 for organic sales.
- $762.50 in Book 4 sales (between the launch and BookFunnel/Story Origin).
- $87.50 in Book 2 and Book 3 sales from BookFunnel/StoryOrigin.

The total is $1,050 in sales.

MONTH 10: SEEMS LIKE A SETBACK

Alas, that $1,000 in sales isn't sustainable when you don't have a book release. You're working on Book 5, but it's still a few months away. And the promos from BookFunnel and StoryOrigin are beginning to attract the same authors with the same readership, so you only add 400 addresses this month.

- $200 in organic sales.
- $100 in sales from Books 2-4 from BookFunnel and StoryOrigin promos.

You make $300 in total sales—even below the month before last. Although this might seem like a setback, it's a normal part of the marketing process. But don't relax just yet: it's time to do something different.

MONTH 11

Now, with four books out and a fifth in pre-order, you decide that it's time for you to start with paid promo newsletters. You dip your toe in with one of the more popular ones: you sign up for a $75 newsletter to promote your Entry Point Novel.

You get 1,000 downloads of your Entry Point Novel, and that results in 50 Book 2 sales, 33 Book 3 sales, and 28 Book 4 sales—115 full-price book sales total.

- Your organic sales get another bump—$250.
- $403 in sales from those 115 units moved by the paid promo newsletter.
- Another $100 from BookFunnel and StoryOrigin promos.

That's $753 for the month (minus the $75 for your paid newsletter promo).

TROUBLESHOOTING: WHAT HAPPENS IF YOUR PAID NEWSLETTER PROMOS DON'T WORK?

Certain promos work much better with some genres than others. If you're writing memoirs, for example, 1,000 downloads with one of the popular $50-$100 promos might not be reasonable. If you're seeing a decent number of downloads with BookFunnel and StoryOrigin, the chances are that the audience for that paid newsletter is just not interested in your genre.

Also, temper your expectations if you're *not* offering a free book. A paid promo to a 99¢ ebook is a significantly steeper hill to climb. The chances are that you won't break even on your sales to your Entry Point Novel, but you may find that your readthrough to Book 2 (which is often significantly higher with a 99¢ Entry Point Novel than a free one) might make up for it. Even so, you likely won't hit that $750+ for the month. You can still see a positive upswing, but your timeline might be longer.

MONTHS 12-15

You're working hard to finish book 5, and you're doing two paid newsletter promos a month now. They're not all winners, but between StoryOrigin, BookFunnel, and the promos, you're averaging 2,000 Entry Point Novels into your readers' hands every month. Your organic sales continue to get juiced by the algorithms as your books' sales stay steady. Some months are better than others, but with a 5% readthrough rate to your Book 2, a two-thirds rate to Book 3, and a 90% rate to Book 4, you're doing well. (If you have the money to pay for a BookBub Featured Deal, this is when you should start applying for those.)

- $250 in organic sales
- $800 in sales from paid promo newsletters, BookFunnel, and StoryOrigin

You hit $1,050 in total sales (minus $100 in Month 12 for BookFunnel annual fee, $70 in Month 15 for StoryOrigin, $40 every month for your mail program, and an average of $80 a month for the paid promo newsletters—about $800 a month net).

MONTH 16

Book 5 is released—and it blows your Book 4 release out of the water. Your pre-orders are the vast majority of your Day 1 sales (although your newsletter announcement doesn't hurt!). You hit 500 orders that first day—just on Book 5 sales—and that grows to 600 over the course of the month. That's over $2,000 in sales on Book 5 alone! You just miss the $3,000 in sales mark for the month after your paid promo newsletters and BookFunnel/StoryOrigin. Your email list hits 7,500. Best of all, you have over $1,000 in profit, even after paying for your editors and cover designer. And by the end of the month, you already have 200 pre-orders for Book 6!

MONTH 17

You decide to do a $150 paid promo newsletter on your full series—and it results in another 1,000 downloads of your Entry Point Novel—but with the full series being promoted, you get 200 sales on Book 2, 133 sales for Book 3, 110 sales on Book 4, and 100 sales on Book 5. This is the first non-release month you've had where you sell more than 500 books.

You start your own BookFunnel promo this month, gathering new authors and getting 500 downloads, resulting in another 100 sales. You hit $2,100 in sales for the month.

MONTH 18+

With five books in your series, your paid promo newsletters and the strength of your newsletter keep you moving more than 350 units every month. Your Book 6 release dwarfs your Book 5 release, and the readthrough to all six books keeps you comfortably above $1,000 in profit.

Now the question is, when will you start your next series?

CAN IT REALLY WORK LIKE THIS?

I admit this is an optimistic timeline, and is calculated for an author who releases three books a year. As mentioned previously, you may need to lengthen this timeline if you're a slower writer. Also, some authors may burn out writing in the same series; I wrote in a completely different genre between Books 4 and 5 in my first series to get my creative juices flowing (but, as you've read, that genre didn't really work out).

This example doesn't include drastic changes in the writing world or your personal life, where something you depend on could go haywire. My personal journey to $1,000 a month took 24 months, not 18—and I was, I believe, fortunate to hit my goals when I did.

But the point is, this should feel attainable, even if you stretch the timeline.

CHAPTER 19
KEEP GOING!

MOST IMPORTANTLY, if you are doing something with your marketing that works well, keep doing it and keep putting effort toward supporting its success—no matter what this book (or any other self-publishing expert) may tell you.

For example, if you have a successful FFIS that's getting you readership to the other books in the series, keep adding books to the series as long as you can create quality products and as long as the readers are there. Being able to release a book, publicize it in your newsletter, and get hundreds (or thousands) of purchases for the week of release is one of the keys to stable author income.

If you have multiple series, try to duplicate what's working with other books. A significant chunk of your readers will follow you to other series if they're in the same genre, and a smaller-but-still-significant group of readers will follow you to related genres as well—as long as you keep setting readers' expectations properly—and meeting them.

Continue to run the promotions that are working every six months (or more or less frequently as your data suggests). When you have extra money, use it to try out new promotions—or uplevel your editing, cover design, and newsletters.

If you try something in your marketing or writing that *doesn't* work, and if you've given it enough time, ask trusted experts—whether it's online writing groups, editors, or people who read your genre—what's wrong. Ask for brutal honesty and do everything you can not to get defensive. There may be a very good reason why you've written your introduction the way you did, but if it's not resonating with your readers, it needs to change. I've heard a lot of brutally honest feedback from editors and early readers. It hurts to get negative feedback, but I'd rather get negative feedback from my editors and early readers than from 100 Amazon reviewers. (And usually the feedback doesn't sting as much a few days later when you think it over—especially if you agree with it!)

Likewise, if you are in love with your cover (or your series title) but it's not working for your audience, it needs to change.

"Keep going" sometimes means changing direction or stopping to fix the problem.

Above all, keep writing, especially when you have something that's working.

Best of luck in your writing careers—and remember, luck favors the prepared!

GLOSSARY

- **Also-boughts**: on a book listing on an online store, this is the list of books near the bottom that readers of the book also purchased.
- **Backlist**: in traditional publishing, this term refers a list of books that a publisher keeps in print, but that aren't newly published. For indie authors, this term means the list of your books that you haven't published recently that are still available for sale. Traditional publishers are usually spending most of their marketing efforts on new releases, but indie authors can spend their marketing efforts promoting their backlists, particularly if their Entry Point Novel hasn't been published recently.
- **Blurb**: most often, authors use this term to refer to the "sales copy" or book description;

usually around 100-200 words, it appears on the book's page on an e-retailer site, and its purpose is to convince the viewer to buy the book; while often confused with a synopsis, a blurb is not intended to summarize the book but rather give the viewer just enough of a taste to compel a purchase.
- **Catalog**: all of the books for sale under one author name.
- **Comps:** short for "comparables," these are books that are similar to yours; "finding your comps" means finding books that are similar to yours so you can target the same audience.
- **Entry Point Novel:** the novel an author uses to get readers interested in the rest of a series or catalog; it can be a FFIS.
- **FFIS**: free first-in-series; the book you give away for free to get people to read the rest of your series (or the rest of your other books).
- **Genre:** the category of your book.
- **ISBNs**: International Standard Book Numbers are 13-digit commercial book identification numbers that are intended to be unique to each edition and variation of a book; for example, an ebook, a paperback, an audiobook, and a hardcover edition of the same book will each have a different ISBN.

- **KU**: An acronym for "Kindle Unlimited," a subscription service offered by Amazon. For indie authors, books that are offered in KU must be enrolled in the Kindle Select program, in which the book must be exclusive to Amazon, and for which authors get paid on page reads by KU subscribers.
- **Overarching arc**: a subplot that extends over multiple books in a series.
- **Paid promo newsletters**: run by for-profit companies, these advertising vehicles sell space in the newsletter to authors to advertise our books, which are usually offered for free, 99¢, or at a significant discount, to all (or a portion of) the company's subscribers.
- **Primary genre:** the main category that readers should find your book in.
- **Rapid-release**: when authors release books in a series quickly; usually, at least three books in the same series will be released within a month of the previous release for the term to apply.
- **Readthrough:** the percentage of readers who go on to read the next book in the series (or the next book in the author's catalog).
- **Series:** a set of books meant to be read as a collection; some books are in series that are meant to be read in order, with overarching

plot and/or character arcs; some books are in series that are connected only by locations or common interests shared by characters (often called **connected standalones**); some series are somewhere in between. Series of books do not always need to be read in order.
- **Standalone:** a book that is not part of a series; it can be read on its own with no connection to other books by that author.
- **Wide**: a term used by indie authors to indicate that their books are not exclusive to Amazon and not enrolled in the KDP Select program (and therefore not available in Kindle Unlimited).

ACKNOWLEDGMENTS

Huge thanks to my *very* early readers Theresa Baumgartner, Jamie Thornton, and G.B. Ralph—and especially my editor Max Christian Hansen. Thanks also to my cover designer Ziad Ezzat of Feral Creative. Thank you to all the early readers and reviewers, including (but not limited to) Dr. Hilary Berwick, A.K. Cotham, Richard Scott Crawford, Michelle Damiani, D.F. Hart, Angela Nurse, Megan Lind Persinger, and Laura Regan.

I could not have written this book without all the advice, wisdom, and lessons dispensed by the book marketing experts who I read, followed, and interviewed: Erin Wright from Wide for the Win, David Gaughran, Mark Leslie Lefebvre, Joanna Penn, Mark Stay, and many others.

Special thanks to Cheryl Shoults, who has been invaluable creating, organizing, and maintaining the Fenway newsletter, website, reader teams, promotions, and a million other items.

To my wife, my children, and my mother: I'm deeply grateful for your encouragement and support, without which my books would never have seen the light of day.

MYSTERY FICTION BY PAUL AUSTIN ARDOIN

The Fenway Stevenson Mysteries

Book One: The Reluctant Coroner

Book Two: The Incumbent Coroner

Book Three: The Candidate Coroner

Book Four: The Upstaged Coroner

Book Five: The Courtroom Coroner

Novella: The Christmas Coroner

Book Six: The Watchful Coroner

Book Seven: The Accused Coroner

Novella: The Clandestine Coroner

Book Eight: The Offside Coroner

Collections

Books 1–3 of The Fenway Stevenson Mysteries

Books 4-6 of The Fenway Stevenson Mysteries

The Woodhead & Becker Mysteries

Book One: The Winterstone Murder

Book Two: The Bridegroom Murder

Book Three: The Trailer Park Murder (*coming soon*)

Dez Roubideaux

Bad Weather

Sign up for *The Coroner's Report,*
Paul Austin Ardoin's fortnightly newsletter:
http://www.paulaustinardoin.com

I hope you found this book helpful in your writing and publishing journey. If you did, I'd sincerely appreciate a review on your favorite book retailer's website, Goodreads, and BookBub. Reviews are crucial for any author, and even just a line or two can make a huge difference.

www.ingramcontent.com/pod-product-compliance
Lightning Source LLC
Chambersburg PA
CBHW030150100526
44592CB00009B/209